THE CENTER FOR CHINESE STUDIES

at the University of California, Berkeley, supported by the Ford Foundation, the Institute of International Studies (University of California, Berkeley), and the State of California, is the unifying organization for social science and interdisciplinary research on contemporary China.

PUBLICATIONS

Wakeman, Frederic, Jr. *Strangers at the Gate: Social Disorder in South China, 1839–1861* (1966)

Townsend, James. *Political Participation in Communist China* (1967)

Potter, J. M. *Capitalism and the Chinese Peasant: Social and Economic Change in a Hong Kong Village* (1968)

Schiffrin, Harold Z. *Sun Yat-sen and the Origins of the Chinese Revolution* (1968)

Schurmann, Franz. *Ideology and Organization in Communist China* (Second Edition, 1968)

Van Ness, Peter. *Revolution and Chinese Foreign Policy: Peking's Support for Wars of National Liberation* (1970)

Larkin, Bruce D. *China and Africa, 1949–1970: The Foreign Policy of the People's Republic of China* (1971)

Schneider, Laurence A. *Ku Chieh-kang and China's New History: Nationalism and the Quest for Alternative Traditions* (1971)

THE
CONSOLIDATION
OF THE
SOUTH CHINA
FRONTIER

*This volume is sponsored by the
Center for Chinese Studies,
University of California, Berkeley*

THE
CONSOLIDATION
OF THE
SOUTH CHINA
FRONTIER

GEORGE V. H. MOSELEY, III

UNIVERSITY OF CALIFORNIA PRESS

BERKELEY, LOS ANGELES, LONDON, 1973

UNIVERSITY OF CALIFORNIA PRESS
BERKELEY AND LOS ANGELES, CALIFORNIA
UNIVERSITY OF CALIFORNIA PRESS, LTD.
LONDON, ENGLAND
COPYRIGHT © 1973, BY
THE REGENTS OF THE UNIVERSITY OF CALIFORNIA
ISBN: 0-520-02102-9
LIBRARY OF CONGRESS CATALOG CARD NUMBER: 73-170719
PRINTED IN THE UNITED STATES OF AMERICA
DESIGNED BY DAVE COMSTOCK

TO MY FATHER AND MOTHER

CONTENTS

PREFACE

THIS study was written as a doctoral dissertation for Oxford University under the supervision of Geoffrey Hudson and was made possible by a three-year scholarship from St. Antony's College (1965–1968) and a one-year travel grant from the Astor Foundation (1966/67), both of which were arranged by the then Warden of the College, F. W. Deakin. It attempts to assess the national-minority policy of the Chinese Communist Party in terms of local data pertaining to a defined and limited area: the south China frontier region. The time span is the decade 1950–1960, supplemented in the last chapter by a broad review of events through early 1970.

Chinese provincial newspapers were the most important source material used. Additional information was culled from the China mainland press generally and from Chinese newspapers published in Hong Kong and southeast Asia. To a limited extent I was able through personal interviews to check facts as reported in the press against the recollections of individuals who had resided in the area during the period under review. In assessing all of this data I was guided less by the theoretical standpoint of any particular discipline than by my earlier experience with minority groups in mainland Southeast Asia and by my previous work on Chinese Communist national-minority policy. It is perhaps for this reason that in the present study I have found myself trying to bring two perspectives into a single focus: the first, discussed in the Introduction, is CCP policy; the second, discussed in chapter 1, is the complex identity of the south China minority peoples. If the subsequent chapters, which trace the interaction between policy and people, suggest that the initiative is usually maintained by Peking, they also reveal that the specific human and physical environment of this frontier does not lend itself to easy manipulation.

For the inspiration to pursue the present study I am largely indebted to my former teacher, Herold Wiens. Frank LeBar, John Musgrave, and Paul Mus also helped me in my early attempt to think imaginatively about the south China frontier. Mr. M. H. Su and his excellent staff (especially Sze To Cheung) at the Universities Service Center in Hong Kong helped me in the collection of material, as did P. K. Tseng and others of the Orientalia Division, Library of Congress. My field trip to northern Thailand, helped financially by the Institute of Current World Affairs, would have been much less rewarding without the personal assistance of Michael Moerman, Kraisri Nimnanhaeminda, and Lee Fan. Regretfully, it seems best to omit the names of persons interviewed, without whose testimony my analysis would have been even thinner than it perhaps is.

THE
CONSOLIDATION
OF THE
SOUTH CHINA
FRONTIER

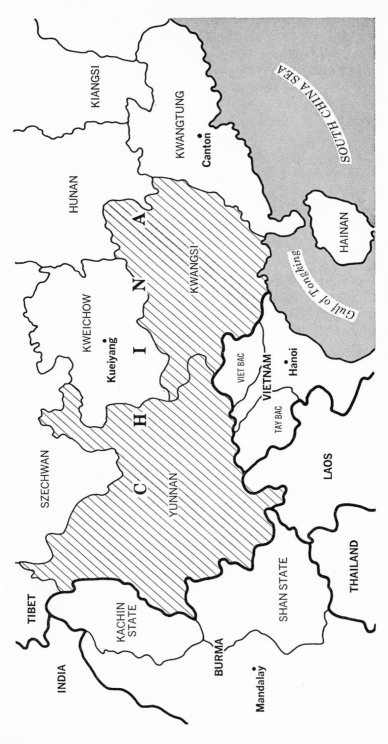

THE SOUTH CHINA FRONTIER REGION IN 1965

INTRODUCTION: CHINESE COMMUNIST NATIONAL MINORITY POLICY

THE People's Republic of China (PRC) includes a wide variety of minority peoples in addition to the predominant Han Chinese. The concentration of the minority peoples (*shao-shu min-tsu*) in the frontier regions of the country is such that they were formerly referred to as "frontier peoples" (*pien-chiang min-tsu*), constituting a veritable ethnic screen around the great agglomerations of Han Chinese in the valleys and plains formed by the country's major rivers. In the high and arid borderlands of Inner Mongolia, Sinkiang, and Tibet, the Han Chinese were themselves in the minority by comparison with the indigenous non-Han peoples. Yunnan and Kwangsi, the two provinces with which the present study is concerned, occupy the southern frontier zone of the PRC from the Himalayas to the Pacific ocean. They lie in a sub-tropical latitude, but extensive mountain systems provide a varied climate. As a result of Han Chinese colonization during the Ming (1368–1644) and Ch'ing (1644–1911) dynasties, as well as during the

Republican era (1911–1949), the proportion of non-Han peoples in Yunnan and Kwangsi fell to one-third of the total population in both provinces. However, the colonists lived in relatively concentrated areas, leaving the more remote upland and border areas in the hands of the minorities: the actual frontier continued to be an ethnically distinct zone which, like the northern and western frontiers of the country, posed a special problem for the Communist authorities.

"Han Chinese" is the standard translation of the Chinese term *han-jen*, which has the literal meaning of "Han people," or simply "Han." Traditionally, it referred to the people of the Han dynasty (206 BC–221 AD) and their descendants, a usage which excluded the Cantonese and other linguistically distinct groups of the southeast coastal region, which came under firm imperial control only in the T'ang dynasty (618–907). During the Ch'ing dynasty (1644–1912), the term *han* was applied to the Chinese of China proper (*pen-ti*) in contradistinction to the peoples of the frontier (*fan-pu*). This usage was continued during the early period of the Republic, the flag of which consisted of five bars representing the Han, the Mongols (*meng*), Tibetans (*tsang*), Turkic Moslems (*hui*), and Manchus (*man*). Use of the term *chung-kuo-jen* (Chinese) was promoted by the Nationalists (1928–1949), who hoped to inculcate individual patriotism irrespective of nationality. For the Chinese Communists (1949–   ), who employ Stalin's definition of "nation" (as determined by common language, territory, economic life, and psychological make-up), the Han are but one of more than fifty national groups in China.[1]

A standard reference book published in Peking lists fifty-four national groups for the whole of China.[2] The Han are first, with 600 million people. The next ten peoples, all of which have populations of over one million, are listed as fol-

[1] One of the most interesting treatments of this question is to be found in Chi Li, *The Formation of the Chinese People* (Cambridge, Mass., 1928), in which the carriers of Chinese culture are designated the "we-group" in contrast to various barbarian peoples who come under the general heading "you-group."

[2] *Jen-min shou-ts'e* (People's Handbook), (Peking, 1965), pp. 115–116.

lows (the names of those significantly represented in Yunnan or Kwangsi are italicized):

Nationality	1957 Population
Mongol	1,640,000
Hui (Chinese Moslem)	3,930,000
Tibetan	2,770,000
Uighur	3,900,000
Miao	2,680,000
Yi (Lolo)	3,260,000
Chuang	7,780,000
Pu-yi	1,310,000
Korean	1,250,000
Manchu	2,430,000

The ordering of this list, which includes all minorities with populations of over one million, may reflect an official view concerning the political importance of these various peoples. The remaining national groups are listed precisely according to size of population. The seventeen peoples with populations of between one million and one hundred thousand are, in descending order (those found in Yunnan or Kwangsi are again italicized), the *T'ung, Yao, Pai (Min-chia),* T'u-chia, *Hani,* Kazakh, *T'ai,* Li, *Lisu, K'awa,* Yü, Kao-shan, *Lahu,* Shui (Shui-chia), Tung-hsiang, *Nahsi,* and *Ching-p'o.* Several of these peoples, like most of those in the first group, possessed developed systems of writing prior to the advent of Communist rule in China, but the smaller peoples listed below, with populations of up to 100,000, were generally illiterate. Similarly, the social organization of the larger groups tended to be feudal, whereas that of the smaller "nationalities" was based on the lineage-group or village. The twenty-six minor national groups are the Kirghiz, T'u, Tahur, *Mo-lao,* Ch'iang, *Pu-lang,* Salar, *Mao-nan,* Ch'i-lao, Sibo, A-ch'ang, Tajik, *P'u-mi, Nu,* Uzbek, Russian, Evenki, *Peng-lung,* Pao-an, Yü-ku, Ching, Tatar, Men-pa, *Tu-lung,* Olunch'un, and Ho-che. Many of these peoples would not be considered nations in the Western sense. Some have been largely assimilated by Han Chinese culture, and most live in a relationship of economic interdependence with the Han Chinese.[3]

Although they represented only six percent of the total population of the country, the area inhabited by the national minorities accounted for sixty percent of the area of the country at the time the PRC was established in 1949. For the most part, they occupied frontier regions of China, often spilling over into adjacent countries. Thus, they were involved in both the foreign and domestic policies of the new state. Frequently, too, ties of religion bound the national minorities with the outside world. During the era of Western colonial and commercial dominance in eastern Asia, the national minority areas of the country were more susceptible to imperialist penetration than were Han Chinese areas.[4]

The Chinese Communists Party (CCP) had developed a specific program to deal with the national minority problem in China. This program was an adaptation of Marxist-Leninist theory on the national question, which had been originally formulated by the Austrian Social-Democrats and then modified by Lenin and Stalin.[5] During its pre-Maoist period of development, the CCP was content to imitate Soviet theory. As early as its Second National Congress of 1922, the CCP proposed that separate republics be formed for the Han, Mongol, Tibetan, and Turkic peoples of China. The demand for a federal state was made even more explicit in the "Constitution of the Soviet Republic of China" promulgated by the CCP in 1931.[6] However, this approach was gradually discarded by

[3] For a critique of the Communist classification of national groups in China, see John DeFrancis, "National and Minority Policies," *Annals of the American Academy of Political and Social Science*, 277 (September 1951): *Report on China*, pp. 146–155.

[4] T'ang Chen-tsung, *Chung-kuo shao-shu min-tsu ti hsin mien-mao* (The new appearance of China' national Minorities), Peking, 1953.

[5] Samad Shaheen, *The Communist (Bolshevik) Theory of National Self-Determination* (The Hague and Bandung, 1956); Richard Pipes, *The Formation of the Soviet Union* (Cambridge, Mass., 1957).

[6] Chang Chih-i, *Chung-kuo ko-ming ti min-tsu wen-t'i ho min-tsu cheng-ts'e chiang-hua (t'i-kang)* (A discussion of the national question in the Chinese revolution and of actual nationalities policy [draft]), (Peking, 1956; translated by George Moseley and published by MIT Press in 1966).

Mao Tse-tung following his attainment of a leading position in the Central Committee in 1935.

With regard to national minority policy, as in several other areas of policy, Mao perceived that what was appropriate in the Soviet context was not necessarily correct for China. In the Maoist revision, anti-imperialism, rather than national self-determination, became the cornerstone of CCP nationalities policy. For Lenin and Stalin, the adherence of the non-Russian peoples to the Bolshevik cause was considered to be an important factor in the revolutionary struggle, whereas in China the seizure of power was almost exclusively a Han Chinese affair. The problem for Mao was to prevent the loss of national minority areas in the course of the revolution.[7]

The nature of the Maoist policy was indicated in CCP declarations of December 20, 1935, and May 25, 1936, addressed, respectively, to the Mongols of Inner Mongolia and the Moslems of northwest China. In these declarations the CCP promised that non-Han peoples who cooperated with the CCP in resisting Japanese aggression and defeating Chiang Kai-shek would be accorded autonomous and equal status in the new China. In other words, "national self-determination" was to extend only to local affairs. According to the CCP, any guarantee of the principle of national independence, including the right of secession, would only be an invitation to the imperialists to detach portions of China: one had to be for China or for imperialism.[8] The Maoist revision of the CCP's national minority policy was not held to be in conflict with Marxism-Leninism, for Lenin's theory of imperialism accorded China—unlike Russia, which was an imperialist state—the status of an oppressed nation. Therefore, the first duty of all nationalities in China was to unite against the foreigners.

The status of national minorities in the PRC is set forth in the *Common Program* (1949) and the *Constitution* (1954), while national minority policy as such is discussed in the *Gen-*

---

[7] For a comparison of Soviet and Chinese Communist national minority policies, see G. F. Hudson, "The Nationalities of China," *St. Antony's Papers*, Vol. 7 (1960), pp. 51–61.

[8] Chang Chih-i, *op. cit.*

*eral Program for the Implementation of Regional Autonomy
for Nationalities in the People's Republic of China* (1952).
These three documents are supplemented and modified by
many other laws and regulations. Articles 50 through 53 of the
Common Program deal with the national minority question:

> ARTICLE 50. All nationalities within the boundaries of the
> People's Republic of China are equal. They shall establish
> unity and mutual aid among themselves, and shall oppose
> imperialism and their own public enemies, so that the
> People's Republic of China will become a big fraternal and
> cooperative family composed of all nationalities. Greater na-
> tionalism and chauvinism shall be opposed. Acts involving
> discrimination, oppression, and splitting of the unity of the
> various nationalities shall be prohibited.
> ARTICLE 51. Regional autonomy shall be exercised in areas
> where national minorities are concentrated and various kinds
> of autonomy organizations of the different nationalities shall
> be set up according to the size of the respective populations
> and regions. In places where different nationalities live to-
> gether and in the autonomous areas of the national minori-
> ties, the different nationalities shall each have an appropriate
> number of representatives in the local organs of political
> power.
> ARTICLE 52. All national minorities within the boundaries
> of the People's Republic of China shall have the right to join
> the People's Liberation Army and to organize local people's
> public security forces in accordance with the unified military
> system of the state.
> ARTICLE 53. All national minorities shall have freedom to
> develop their dialects and languages, to preserve or reform
> their traditions, customs, and religious beliefs. The People's
> Government shall assist the masses of the people of all na-
> tional minorities to develop their political, economic, cul-
> tural, and educational construction work.[9]

The general principles relating to the national minorities
which are stated in the *Common Program* are reaffirmed and

[9] "The Common Program of the Chinese People's Political Consultative Conference (CPPCC)," in *The Important Documents of the First
Plenary Session of the CPCC* (Peking, 1949).

elaborated in the *Constitution*, Article 3 of which declares that "The People's Republic of China is a unified, multinational state" in which "all nationalities are equal." Areas "entirely or largely inhabited by national minorities" are to enjoy regional autonomy, but "national autonomous areas are inalienable parts of the People's Republic of China." According to Article 54, organs of self-government in national minority areas may be established at three levels: *ch'ü* (region), *chou* (prefecture), *hsien* (county). The smaller nationality *hsiang* (townships) do not exercise full autonomy but may "take specific measures suited to the characteristics of the nationalities concerned" (Article 60). The national minorities are to be represented not only in their local people's congresses, but also in the National People's Congress, in which the 1953 *Electoral Law* guarantees them at least 150 seats, more than twice the number to which they would be entitled on a proportional basis. The *Constitution* also provides that a Nationalities Committee be set up under the National People's Congress. This committee is entirely separate from the Nationalities Affairs Commission of the State Council, the highest administrative body of the PRC.[10]

The *General Program for the Implementation of Regional Autonomy* specifies that joint autonomous regimes may be established in areas shared by two or more comparatively large national minorities, while in areas inhabited by one large and several smaller nationalities the latter must be accorded separate national autonomy within the larger autonomous unit established for the major group. Han Chinese are precluded from exercising regional autonomy, even if they form a minority within an autonomous region of another nationality, the presumption being that the rights of Han Chinese do not need special protection. The organs of local authority of the autonomous areas are established "according to the basic principles of democratic centralism and the system of people's congresses." That is, the people participate in the execution

[10] "Constitution of the People's Republic of China (PRC)," in *Documents of the First Session of the First National Congress of the PRC* (Peking, 1955).

of decisions made by higher authority. Although it is made clear that the national minorities are to advance toward socialism along with the Han Chinese, the *General Program* stipulates that "internal reforms shall be carried out in a national autonomous region in accordance with the wishes of the majority of its people and of the local leaders who are associated with the people."[11]

The programmatic nature of the PRC's national minority policy was stated clearly by Liu Shao-ch'i in his *Report on the Draft Constitution*:

> The building of a socialist society is the common objective of all nationalities within our country. Only socialism can guarantee to each and every nationality a high degree of economic and cultural development. Our state has a duty to help all nationalities within the country to take this path step by step to happiness.

Marxism-Leninism makes it incumbent upon the Han Chinese majority to assist the fraternal nationalities in their march toward socialism. As Liu observes,

> For historical reasons the Han nationality has a comparatively higher political, economic, and cultural level than the others. But this by no means entitles it to any special privileges or to put on airs toward its brother nationalities. On the contrary, it has a special obligation to help all the brother nationalities in their development. Although all the national minorities have won their right to national equality, they cannot immediately overcome their original economic and cultural backwardness simply by their own strength and in their present circumstances. It is therefore very important for the Han nationality to help them. The Han people must give their sincere and devoted assistance in the economic and cultural fields to their brother nationalities.

Liu goes on to warn against the twin errors of chauvinism on the part of the Han Chinese and nationalism on the part

[11] "General Program of the People's Republic of China for the Implementation of Regional Autonomy for Nationalities," in *Policy Towards Nationalities of the PRC* (Peking, 1953), pp. 1–13.

of the minorities, both of which may endanger the "unity among the nationalities." Finally, Liu points out that the different nationalities in China will not necessarily "arrive at socialism at the same time and by the same means."

> Socialist transformation among certain national minorities will begin rather later and may take more time than in areas where the Han people live. By the time socialist transformation is under way among these national minorities, the work of building socialism will probably have achieved big successes in most parts of the country. By then conditions for socialist transformation among these national minorities will be more favorable, because by that time the state will have greater material strength to help them. The masses of the people of the national minorities will also be willing to take this path once they see the benefits of the victory of socialism throughout the country. . . ."[12]

Thus, apart from aiding the PRC in attaining the objectives of national unity and security, the policy of regional autonomy was designed to enable the regime to isolate relatively backward areas inhabited by national minorities. "Socialist transformation" could be delayed there even beyond the time when the rest of the country would have entered into the more advanced stage of "building socialism." Han Chinese interference in national minority affairs is justified in terms of helping the fraternal nationalities in progressing toward socialism. Actually, the evolution of the national minorities within the PRC is entirely in the hands of the Chinese Communist Party, in the organization of which no concession is made to any regional particularity. Members of the national minorities are permitted, even encouraged, to join the CCP, but in doing so they simply become agents of the Han Chinese for the transformation of their own peoples.

In its actual implementation, the policy of regional autonomy does not mean that the national minorities can them-

---

[12] Liu Shao-ch'i, "Report on the Draft Constitution of the People's Republic of China," delivered at the First Session of the First National People's Congress of the PRC, September 15, 1954, and published in *Documents*, etc., Peking, 1955.

selves dispose of the autonomous areas, of which they are theoretically masters, as they see fit. In practice, the PRC seems to recognize only the right of cultivators to work the land on which they are dependent, whether as individuals or as members of cooperatives. Han Chinese have not displaced the non-Han peoples from their farm lands. But in all other respects the frontier regions have been thrown open to exploitation by the state irrespective of whether they lie within or outside of national autonomous areas. This would certainly have occurred under any Chinese government dedicated to the modernization of the country. However, the PRC's national minority policy, designed to soften the impact of the state on the non-Han peoples in the mountains and on the frontiers, has insisted upon their theoretical right to equality and cultural autonomy.[13]

[13] A fuller presentation of documentary materials relating to the national minority question in China may be found in Henry G. Schwarz, *Chinese Policies Toward Minorities* (Western Washington State College, 1971).

I

THE SITUATION
OF NATIONAL
MINORITIES
IN YUNNAN
AND KWANGSI

THE GEOGRAPHICAL SETTING

S OUTH China and northern Southeast Asia form an ecological unit which has been relatively stable for at least
two thousand years. The traditional culture of the majority
of the people of south China, like that of the Vietnamese,
Thai, Lao, and Burmese, depends on wet-rice agriculture. In
this culture, the run-off of the monsoon rains is regulated so
as to inundate the rice fields and keep them flooded during the
growing season. The fertility of the soil is maintained by de-
posits of alluvium brought by the annual flooding. The plow,
characteristically drawn by a water buffalo, is utilized for pre-
paring the fields for sowing. Because of its dependence on
suitably level terrain, the spread of this wet-rice culture has

been severely limited by geographical factors. Divergent cultures persist in the upland areas which it could not penetrate, while poor communications have tended to isolate wet-rice cultivators who inhabit small valleys and basins physically remote from the main centers of population. The political strength of the states which grew up in this area varied according to the extent of their rice lands, the smaller normally being dependent on the larger.

The culture of the upland areas was traditionally based on slash-and-burn agriculture. In this mode of cultivation, the forest or secondary growth is periodically cut and burned, after which dry rice or maize is planted by means of a digging stick. The fertility of the soil depends on the burning of the vegetation and is soon exhausted. After one or a few crops have been harvested, the land must be allowed to lie fallow for a number of years. For this reason, fire-field agriculture cannot sustain nearly so dense a population as can the flooded-field agriculture of the lowlander; normally, the uplander has been politically dependent on the lowlander.[1] In the high, narrow valleys that provide a transitional zone between upland and lowland agriculture, the same people may practice both irrigated and dry farming. The terracing of hillsides for wet-rice agriculture provides another link between the two.[2]

The southern frontier of China slices through the midsection of this ecological unit with its lowland and upland varieties of agriculture. Yunnan and Kwangsi, China's southernmost provinces, stretch from the sea to the Tibetan highlands. (Kwangsi ceased being a landlocked province in 1965, when its southeastern border was extended to the Gulf of

---

[1] This contrast is exhibited dramatically in Tongking, where the Red River delta's 15,000 square kilometers support a population of 7,500,000, while 102,000 square kilometers of adjacent upland country supports a population of only 800,000. Pierre Gourou, "Land Utilization in Upland Areas of Indochina," in *The Development of Upland Areas in the Far East* (New York: International Secretariat, Institute of Pacific Relations, 1951), II, 31.

[2] Pierre Gourou, *L'Asie* (Paris, 1953); George B. Cressey, *Asia's Lands and Peoples* (New York, 1963).

Tongking, thereby incorporating the protrusion of Kwangtung from the Luichow peninsula to the Vietnamese frontier.)
Geographically, the two provinces are tilted, with elevations
rising steadily from southeast to northwest. The plateau of
eastern Yunnan is situated at about 2,000 meters. The mountains to the northwest rise to over 3,000 meters, while to the
southeast the Yunnan plateau gives way to hilly country which
descends to the plateau of eastern Kwangsi, lying between 200
and 300 meters. Most of Kwangsi is drained by the West River,
which flows through Kwangtung to the sea; the boundary between Kwangsi and Vietnam approximates the watershed
between the West and the Red River drainage systems. The
geographical orientation of Yunnan is in sharp contrast to
that of Kwangsi, for it is drained primarily by rivers which
flow southward out of China. The extreme western portion of
the province is traversed from north to south by the Salween,
while the Mekong cuts across the province from northwest to
south. Eastern Yunnan is served by the Red and Black Rivers.
Only the northern fringe of the province, which is drained by
the Yangtze, together with a strip of territory on the east, connected with Kwangsi by the upper reaches of the West River,
have riverine connections with the rest of China.[3]

Plains and basins take up one-fifth of the area of Kwangsi,
the remaining four-fifths being occupied by hills and mountains. Only about 10 percent of the area of the province is
cultivated, however, and most of this is in the low-lying eastern plain. Double cropping is the rule on this plain, which
enjoys a tropical climate and abundant rainfall. Its population
density varies between 200 and 300 per square kilometer as
compared with 50 for northwestern Kwangsi, which has a
cooler climate and a less reliable summer monsoon. Upland
and lowland Kwangsi are connected by the Yu-chiang and
other rivers which feed the West River. Along the valleys of
these rivers the favorable climatic features of the southeastern
part of the province, together with the comparatively high

[3] Chang Chi-yun (ed.), *National Atlas of China*, Vol. IV: *South China*
(Taipei, 1962).

population densities which they make possible, penetrate deeply into the mountainous northwest.[4]

Forests cover 20 percent of the area of Yunnan, as compared with only 7.5 percent for Kwangsi. This is due mainly to heavier precipitation in Yunnan and secondarily to the fact that large expanses of Yunnan's mountains are too precipitous or too high to permit slash-and-burn agriculture. Yunnan's highest mountains are in the extreme northwest, where the upper reaches of the Salween, Mekong, and Yangtze Rivers approach one another. The deep gorges cut by the southward-flowing Salween and Mekong are the dominant terrain features of western Yunnan, while the eastward-flowing Yangtze defines most of the province's northern border. The ravines of the Red and Black Rivers separate the plateau of central Yunnan from the hilly lowlands in the southwest. These rift valleys, which may be several thousand feet deep, pose great obstacles to communications. Only about 5 percent of Yunnan's surface is cultivated: 27 percent of the cultivated area is sown to rice, of which less than 10 percent is upland, or dry rice. The Tali Plain, in the west-central part of the province, is a largely self-contained agricultural and commercial center of considerable importance in the life of the province. The climate of the southern fringe of Yunnan, like that of southeastern Kwangsi, is tropical. The prevalence of malaria in the low-lying valleys of this region has, until recently, prevented full exploitation of its rich potential. The southeastern corner of Yunnan, east of the Red River, is hilly country similar to adacent parts of Kwangsi.[5]

CHINESE EXPANSION INTO YUNNAN AND KWANGSI

Chinese interest in Yunnan is as old as the Han dynasty, during which time there flourished an overland trade route through the southwest to India. T'ien, the local principality

[4] JPRS (US Department of Commerce, Joint Publications Research Service) 14954, a translation of Sun Ching-chih, *Hua-nan ti-ch'ü ching-chi ti-li* (Economic Geography of the South China region), (Peking, 1959).

[5] JPRS 15069, a translation of Sun Ching-chih, *Hsi-nan ti-ch'ü ching-chi ti-li* (Economic Geography of the Southwest China Region), (Peking, 1960).

which controlled most of the province, recognized the over-
lordship of Han. In the fourth century T'ien was conquered
by Szechwan, which was under the control of one of the Three
Kingdoms then dominating China. The T'ang dynasty,
strongly oriented toward the northwest route to the outside
world, did not control Yunnan, then constituted as the state
of Nan-chao. Nan-chao was not subdued until the Mongols
invaded Yunnan in the thirteenth century. With the defeat
of Nan-chao, the local T'ai elite fled southward, eventually
forming a new state at Sukhodaya in present-day Thailand.

Chinese political control came earlier to Kwangsi than it
did to Yunnan. The kingdom of Nan-yüeh, which controlled
the entire stretch of coastal lowlands from the mouth of the
West River at present-day Canton to the Red River delta in
Tongking, was conquered by the Han dynasty. Under the
T'ang dynasty, this whole region was governed as a single unit,
called Ling-nan. The distinction between lowland and upland
Kwangsi was given administrative recognition by the Sung
(960–1127), which placed the mountainous western part of
the province under separate administration. Although Kwangsi and Yunnan were fully incorporated into the empire by the
Sung and Mongol dynasties, respectively, it was only under the
Ming that they were given provincial boundaries like those of
today. During the Ch'ing dynasty, Yunnan and Kweichow
(*yün-kuei*, as they are commonly abbreviated in Chinese) were
placed under a single viceroy, while another viceroy was given
responsibility for the two provinces of Kwangtung and
Kwangsi (*liang-kuang*, "the two *kuang*").[6]

Preceeded by many centuries of Chinese political and cultural influence, large numbers of Han settlers began entering
Kwangsi and Yunnan during the Ming dynasty. The principal
route into Yunnan was from Szechwan, to the north. Thus,
the bulk of the Han Chinese in Yunnan are speakers of
Mandarin Chinese. In Kwangsi, on the other hand, most Han

[6] C. P. Fitzgerald, *China, A Short Cultural History* (3rd ed., London,
1965); Albert Hermann, *Historical and Commercial Atlas of China*,
Harvard-Yenching Institute, Monograph Series, Vol. I (1935; reprint,
Taipei, 1964).

Chinese speak Cantonese, but there is an important Mandarin-speaking enclave in the north, around Kweilin. The latter represents immigration from Hunan, whereas the Cantonese-speaking population originated in Kwangtung.

Han Chinese colonization of Yunnan and Kwangsi was an extension into new areas of an existing pattern of civilization. Being primarily wet-rice cultivators, the colonists sought level, well-watered ground where irrigation would be relatively easy. This they found in the lowlands of Kwangsi, including the interior river valleys, and on the plateau of Yunnan. Scattered here and there amidst the expanse of rice fields were towns and cities which had economic and political ties with Szechwan, Kweichow, Hunan, and Kwangtung. These urban centers were the focal points of the new settlement areas. The Han settlers shunned regions that were geographically inhospitable to the cultural pattern with which they were familiar. Malarial conditions that had once existed in lowland Kwangsi had been eliminated at an earlier date, but persisted in the valleys of southern and western Yunnan, effectively barring Han Chinese settlement; the hills and mountains of both provinces remained virtually untouched. Thus, the area of Han Chinese settlement in Yunnan and Kwangsi was restricted despite the fact that the colonizers had become numerically predominant well before the Communist era. The Kweichow plateau was colonized even more slowly than Yunnan, with which it is geographically related.

The colonization of Yunnan and Kwangsi began the climactic phase of the two-thousand-year-old southward push of the Han Chinese. Before the establishment of the empire in 221 BC, most of south China, including the middle Yangtze valley, was inhabited by T'ai peoples, while in the north the future Han Chinese nation was developing in the central plain (*chung-yüan*, from which derives the idea of *chung-kuo*, or Middle Kingdom), where agriculture was favored by the rich alluvial soil deposited by the Yellow River. Even in this cradle of Chinese civilization there existed minorities which were difficult to assimilate. As Professor Dubbs has noted: "During the first millenium BC, the civilized Chinese inhabited the valleys and plains of north China, but the hills, forests, and marshes were occupied by barbarian tribes, whom the Chinese did not conquer until 300 BC."[7] These Chinese used cattle for draft purposes and raised millet and kaoliang, whereas the T'ai in the south used the water buffalo and grew rice.[8] Alone among the peoples with whom the early Chinese had contact, the T'ai were not regarded as barbarians (man). They possessed a state system scarcely less sophisticated than that of the early Chinese, and in the cultural realm they were known for sericulture and bronze casting.

In the post-Han period, large-scale Chinese emigration to the Yangtze valley was stimulated by barbarian invasions of the north China plain. A southern Chinese culture became fully formed during the Sung dynasty, which (after 1126) had its seat in the Yangtze valley. The Sung also prepared the way for the colonization of the West River valley by crushing a major Chuang rising in Kwangtung. The Chuang people had been formed by the combination of the indigenous population (yüeh) of southeast coastal China with a T'ai upper strata. The T'ai element had moved southward as a result of Han Chinese pressure in the Yangtze valley. The Chuang occupied the rice-producing lowlands at the time of the Han Chinese influx. In Yunnan, the Han Chinese settlers found the central plateau area occupied by a T'ai-led indigenous population, in this case the Yi (formerly called Lolo, or pai-i).[9]

THE DISTRIBUTION OF NON-HAN PEOPLES

Han Chinese colonization led to the displacement, absorption, or acculturation of a large proportion of the plateau-dwelling Yi of Yunnan and the lowland-dwelling Chuang of Kwangsi. For the most part, this process was peaceful. The

[7] H. H. Dubbs, "The Concept of Unity in China," in The Quest for Political Unity in World History, ed. by Stanley Pargellis; Annual Report of the American Historical Association, 1942, III (Washington, 1944), 3–19.

[8] George B. Cressey, China's Geographic Foundations (New York and London, 1934).

[9] Herold J. Wiens, China's March Toward the Tropics (Hamden, Conn., 1954).

Han Chinese brought with them a superior culture which was readily adopted by other wet-rice cultivators. Distinguishing characteristics of Han Chinese agricultural technique included use of the iron plow, the transplanting of rice seedlings, the application of manure, and superior irrigation works. Moreover, the Han Chinese were harder workers than the indigenous populations. Where the Yi harvested one crop a year, the Han Chinese introduced double-cropping; where the Chuang harvested two crops a year, the Han realized three. The indigenous peoples were also impressed by the literary, bureaucratic, military, and commercial qualities of Chinese civilization, which, until the arrival of the Europeans, had no peer. By adopting Chinese language and dress, large numbers of Yi and Chuang "became" Chinese.[10] Individuals of both Yi and Chuang ancestry rose to high official positions.

Notwithstanding the absorptive power of Han Chinese life, however, the assimilation of indigenous wet-rice cultivators in Yunnan and Kwangsi was far from complete when the PRC was established in 1949. Yi and Chuang villages continued to co-exist with Han Chinese villages on the plateau of Yunnan and the lowlands of Kwangsi, respectively. In the river valleys of western Kwangsi, and along the Yu-chiang in particular, the Chuang remained in possession of most of the area which was suitable for flooded-field agriculture. The Han Chinese here limited themselves to acquiring an important economic position based on such commercial centers as Pai-se. The upland river valleys of Kwangsi afforded the Chuang a degree of natural protection against Han Chinese colonization which was not available to the lowland Chuang. An even more formidable natural obstacle enabled the Min-chia of Yunnan to preserve their identity. The Min-chia inhabit the Tali Plain in the west-central part of Yunnan. This fertile area is surrounded by high mountains which are pierced by only two passes, one to the north and one to the south. For a quite different reason, the southern fringe of Yunnan remained the preserve of the T'ai. The anopheles mosquito thrived in the warm and humid

[10] Inez de Beauclair, "Ethnic Groups," in *A General Handbook of China*, (New Haven: Human Relations Area Files, [about] 1956).

river valleys in this area and, unlike the T'ai, the Han Chinese had not developed a natural resistance to malaria.[11]

The relationship between the Han Chinese settlers and the hill farmers was altogether different from their relationship with other flooded-field agriculturalists. The Han Chinese did not covet the steeply inclined lands of the hill farmer, while the latter found comparatively little in Chinese culture which was of practical use to him. Because Han Chinese and hill farmer did not confront one another on a common ecological footing, intermarriage and assimilation occurred only rarely. The hill farmer could not "become" Chinese without abandoning his mode of existence. Occasionally, Han Chinese did become hill farmers, but in so doing they cut themselves off from Chinese culture just as, in the far north of China, Han Chinese who took up livestock herding in imitation of the Central Asian pastoralists thereby ceased to be Han Chinese.[12]

Economic exploitation of the hill farmers by unscrupulous Han Chinese traders, together with the natural proclivity of the upland tribesmen to raid lowland communities, largely account for the fact that, historically, the Chinese went to war much more frequently against the uplander than they did against the lowlander. The pattern of Han Chinese colonization in Yunnan and Kwangsi is part of the larger pattern of Chinese expansion over thousands of years from the cradle of Chinese civilization in the Yellow River valley. In the course of this expansion, the Chinese were fused with other peoples following a similar mode of livelihood, a process which accounts for the marked divergence of dialect and physical type among the Han Chinese of today. As Professor Fitzgerald has said, "The Chinese are less a nation than a fusion of peoples united by a common culture, and the history of China is the record of an expanding culture."[13] Peoples whose mode of existence contrasted sharply with that of the Han Chinese

[11] Frank M. LeBar, Gerald C. Hickey, and John K. Musgrave, *Ethnic Groups of Mainland Southeast Asia* (New Haven, 1964). The coverage of this volume includes Yunnan and Kwangsi.

[12] *Cf.* Owen Lattimore, *Inner Asian Frontiers of China* (New York, 1940).

[13] Fitzgerald, *op. cit.*, p. 1.

were not generally amalgamated into Chinese culture but retained their distinctive identity. They constituted, as has been aptly observed, "geographical minorities."[14] The major "geographical minorities" of north and west China were the Mongol, Turkic, and Tibetan herders; in south China, they were the slash-and-burn agriculturalists.

The principal hill peoples of Kwangsi are the Miao and Yao.[15] Both of these peoples have been neighbors of the Han Chinese since ancient times, having gradually descended from north China. Their present distribution is as follows (population figures based on 1953 census):

	Miao	Yao
Kweichow	1,425,000	
Hunan	378,000	
Yunnan	360,000	
Kwangsi	204,000	469,000
Szechwan	84,000	
Kwangtung		41,000
Total	2,451,000	510,000

The Miao and Yao extend into Vietnam, Laos, and even northern Thailand, but they are more numerous inside China than they are south of the border. The principal occupation of the Miao and the Yao is fire-field agriculture. In most Yao villages there is some knowledge of Chinese writing, while an acquaintance with spoken Chinese is common among the Miao. More so than the Yao, the Miao have struggled tenaciously to maintain their independence; on several occasions they rose up against the Ch'ing dynasty.[16] Miao and Yao villages are found throughout much of the upland regions of Kwangsi. They are generally widely scattered, but in several places they are sufficiently concentrated to have made it feasi-

[14] Ma Ch'ang-shou, "Shao-shu min-tsu wen-t'i" (The National Minority Question), *Min-tsu-hsüeh yen-chiu chi-k'an* (Ethnological Research), VI (Chungking, 1948).

[15] Unless otherwise indicated, the ethnographic data in this section is taken from LeBar, Hickey, and Musgrave, *op. cit.*

[16] F. M. Savina, *Histoire des Miao* (Hong Kong, 1930).

ble for the CCP to establish autonomous areas. Although the two peoples do not intermingle, the Miao and Yao languages are closely related; taken together, they form a separate linguistic group within the Sino-Tibetan family of languages.

The hill peoples of Yunnan belong to several different ethno-linguistic groups. The Tibeto-Burmans—represented by the Yi, Ching-p'o, Nahsi, Lisu, Lahu Min-chia, and Hani—are the most important. The Yi are both plains and hill people, while the Min-chia are exclusively wet-rice cultivators. The Lsiu and Nahsi depend heavily on animal husbandry. They are situated in the far northwest of Yunnan, on the fringe of Tibet. The Min-chia spread north and west from Tali, forming an ethnic frontier between, on the one hand, the Lisu and Nahsi further to the north and, on the other, the Yi and Chinese on the Yunnan plateau. The Yi of Yunnan are an offshoot of the Yi of adjacent parts of Szechwan, where their fierce resistance to Chinese control earned them the title, "the independent Lolo of Ta-liang-shan." Ta-liang-shan is the mountain fastness in southern Szechwan which was the homeland of the Yi, or Lolo.[17] The Hani, found on the Sino-Vietnamese frontier, are closely related to the Yi.

Speakers of Mon-Khmer languages found among the hill peoples of Yunnan are represented by the K'awa (Wa) and Pu-lang, located in the southern part of the province. The K'awa occupy a large bloc of territory lying mainly in Burma but extending across the Chinese border into Yunnan. Like the Yi in Szechwan, the K'awa have fought tenaciously to guard their independence. Their reputation for headhunting helped to keep officials out of their area during the period of British rule in Burma, and it was only slowly that Chinese Communist cadres were able to penetrate their territory in southwest Yunnan.[18] The Pu-lang in Yunnan are also but a fragment of a larger ethnic group found mainly in Burma.

[17] Lin Yueh-hwa, *The Lolo of Liang Shan* (New Haven, 1961), a translation of Lin's *Liang-shan i-chia* (Shanghai, 1947). C. P. Fitzgerald, *The Tower of Five Glories: A Study of the Min Chia of Ta Li, Yunnan* (London, 1941).

[18] G. E. Harvey, "The Wa People of the Burma-China Frontier," *St. Antony's Papers*, No. 2 (London, 1957), pp. 126–135.

The Pu-lang have a total population of no more than two hundred thousand, counting those in Burma and Thailand as well as those in China, whereas there are some three hundred thousand K'awa in Yunnan alone. The K'awa and Pu-lang are primarily fire-field agriculturalists. These two peoples are the northernmost representatives of an Austroasiatic ethnic strain which, extending through Laos, dominates the high plateau of south Vietnam.

The approximate populations of upland peoples in Yunnan and Kwangsi at time of 1953 census (rounded to nearest 10,000) were:

	Yunnan	Kwangsi
Miao	360,000	200,000
Yao		470,000
Ching-p'o	110,000	
Nahsi	150,000	
Lisu	320,000	
Lahu	170,000	
Yi	1,500,000	
Hani	270,000	
K'awa	280,000	
Pu-lang	40,000	

Of these upland groups, the Han Chinese have had longest contact with the Miao and Yao. The various Tibeto-Burman groups are also relatively familiar. Most different from the Han Chinese, as measured by language and physical type, are the Mon-Khmer speakers. As will be shown, however, the conventional anthropological classification according to linguistic categories is less important in contemporary Chinese politics than is the differentiation according to land use. Leach has demonstrated this fact in a case study of a comparable situation in northern Burma, where the upland Kachin confront the lowland Shan.[19] The relations of one community of fire-field cultivators with the Han Chinese tends to be like the relations

[19] E. R. Leach, *Political Systems of Highland Burma* (London, 1964); "The Frontiers of Burma," *Comparative Studies in Society and History*, III, 1 (1960), 49–68.

of any other dry-farming community with the Han Chinese. Another set of relations obtain between the Han Chinese and peoples, such as the Nahsi and Lisu, who are primarily livestock herders. As a way of life, animal husbandry is further removed from the pattern of Chinese civilization than is hill farming. Cultivators of dry and paddy rice have this in common: the proportion of animal products in their diet is negligible. They are essentially vegetarians, with pigs and fowl being killed and eaten only on special occasions. It is just the reverse with the livestock herders, for whom meat and milk are staple dietary items.[20]

In the same way, Han Chinese relations with other wet-rice agriculturalists are of a quite different type than those with upland peoples. In describing the peoples of Southeast Asia (where animal husbandry of the almost pure type encountered on the fringes of Tibet does not occur), contemporary anthropologists refer to the uplanders as "hill tribes," reserving the label "minorities" for lowlanders who are ethnically distinct from the dominant national group.[21] Actually, the socio-political organization of the slash-and-burn agriculturalists seldom attains tribal dimensions, the village being the most common unit of identification. Because their area of habitation is less broken up by lowland agriculturalists, the livestock herders of the Tibetan massif, including northwest Yunnan and western Szechwan, frequently surpass the hill tribes in political organization. Thus, for instance, the Khamba of eastern Tibet, thanks to strong tribal links, have demonstrated their capacity for self-defense even against the Chinese Communists.

The population density of Yunnan is only half that of Kwangsi. At the time of the 1953 census, Yunnan, with 436,-200 square kilometers, had a population of 17,472,737, whereas Kwangsi, with only 220,400 square kilometers, had a population of 19,560,822.[22] Of the two provinces' combined

[20] Pierre Gourou, "The Development of Upland Areas in China," in *The Development of Upland Areas in the Far East*, I (1949), 1–25.

[21] Peter Kunstadter (ed.), *Southeast Asian Tribes, Minorities, and Nations* (2 vols., Princeton, 1967), especially his introduction, I, 3–72.

[22] S. Chandrasekhar, *China's Population* (Hong Kong, 1959).

population of 37 million, 24 million, or approximately two-thirds, are "native Chinese speakers." The bulk of the remaining 13 million people are T'ai speakers, the Chuang alone accounting (in 1953) for roughly 6.5 million. Small numbers of T'ung, another T'ai group, are found along the Kwangsi-Kweichow border. The T'ai in Yunnan, including the "Chinese Shans," the Nüa, and the T'ai Lü, had a 1953 population of more than half a million. Although the T'ai are numerically less important in Yunnan than in Kwangsi, their position on the frontier and their trans-frontier links make the T'ai of Yunnan at least equal to the Chuang in political importance. The T'ai-speaking groups of northern Vietnam, the most important of which is the Tho, are almost completely isolated from the main T'ai agglomerations in the Mekong (Lao), Menam (Thai), and Salween (Shan) basins to the west. These western groups, like the T'ai in Yunnan, are Buddhists, whereas the eastern T'ai, including those in Kwangsi and Vietnam, are not. Eastern T'ai also extend into Kweichow, where they are usually referred to as Pu-yi or Chung-chia.[23]

It is almost impossible to convey an adequate impression of the ethnic complexity of Kwangsi and, more particularly, of Yunnan. The accompanying map can only indicate the limits of habitation of the different major groups without showing the complicated way in which they overlap. It is based on a map recently prepared at Yale University[24] which marks a great advance over anything previously available in English, but is less detailed than some which have been published in the Soviet Union.[25] What these maps cannot show is the *altitudinal* distribution of ethnic groups, which makes it possible for several peoples, in distinct strata, to inhabit a single territorial unit. For example, in a hilly area which might be nomi-

[23] William C. Dodd, *The Tai Race* (Cedar Rapids, Mich., 1923); Erik Seidenfaden, *The Thai Peoples* (Bangkok, 1963).

[24] "Ethnolinguistic Groups of Mainland Southeast Asia," compiled by Frank M. LeBar, Gerald O. Hickey, and John K. Musgrave (New Haven: Human Relations Area Files, 1964), to accompany *Ethnic Groups of Mainland Southeast Asia.*

[25] S. I. Bruk, *Karta Narodov Kitaia, MNR i Korei* (Moscow, 1959), and *Atlas Narodov Mira* (Moscow, 1964), Plate 49.

ETHNOLINGUISTIC GROUPS OF YUNNAN AND KWANGSI

Tibeto-Burman

Tai

Mon-Khmer in Western Yunnan;
Miao-Yao in Eastern Yunnan and Kwangsi

Han Chinese predominate elsewhere

nally T'ai or Han Chinese, these wet-rice farmers would only occupy the valleys, leaving the higher elevations to slash-and-burn agriculturalists, or simply uninhabited.[26] These peoples would have economic relations with one another, centering on a periodic market held at a town or village in the domain of the wet-rice cultivator. Market day was thus an ethnic pageant, with the various tribal people descending from the surrounding hills to exchange their produce for articles of daily use.

Policy toward minorities before 1949

Chinese suzerainty in Kwangsi and Yunnan, firmly established only in Sung and Yuan times, was threatened by Western encroachment during the hundred years preceding the establishment of the PRC. The fact that the Taiping rebellion (1850–1864), with its Christian messianism, had arisen in Kwangsi was a measure of the outside influence felt in the province. As the Taiping rebellion flared across the rest of south China, Yunnan was convulsed by a great Moslem uprising which lasted nearly twenty years (1855–1873). Although the Moslems certainly had their own grievances against the Manchus who ruled China, it is also true that they received arms by way of Burma and, in 1872, even despatched a mission to London in the hope of securing help from Britain, already implicated in another Moslem rebellion (1862–1873) that was laying waste to northwest China. French arms were used by the viceroy of Yunnan and Kweichow in his pacification of the Moslem uprising in Yunnan: the population of the province dropped from 16 million prior to the rebellion to 6 million following it.[27]

The suppression of these revolts was followed by yet more persistent foreign penetration into Yunnan and Kwangsi. Subsequent to China's defeat in the Sino-French war of 1884/5,

[26] The altitudinal factor in human settlement in this part of the world is brought out by Chi-yun Chang, "Climate and Man in China," *Annals of the Association of American Geographers*, XXXVI, 1 (March 1946), 44–73.
[27] John K. Fairbank and Ssu-Yu Teng, *Ch'ing Administration*, Harvard-Yenching Institute Studies, Vol. VI (Cambridge, Mass., 1960).

France established a sphere of influence across the southern fringe of China contiguous to its colonial domain in Indochina.[28] The British, based in Burma and Hong Kong, competed with the French for influence in Yunnan and Kwangsi. The annexation of upper Burma in 1886 excited British interest in the commercial penetration of Yunnan. Before the turn of the century, the Kwangsi cities of Lungchow, Nanning, and Weichow, all of which are served by river transport, were opened to foreign traders. By 1889, Teng-chung, Meng-tze, and Sze-mao in Yunnan were similarly opened, and in 1910 a rail link between Kunming and Hanoi was completed. One of the few checks on Anglo-French aggressiveness in Yunnan and Kwangsi was the long-standing rivalry between these two colonial powers. This rivalry led to an agreement in 1896 which recognized the Mekong River as the boundary between the French-occupied Lao state of Luang Prabang, claimed by both Annam and Siam, and British-occupied Kengtung, the eastern Shan state which had been a tributary of both China and Burma.[29] Another restraint operating on representatives in the field such as August Pavie of France and George Scott of Britain was the reluctance of their home governments to be drawn into hostilities with China, which would jeopardize their commercial interests in other parts of the Middle Kingdom. The decadent Ch'ing dynasty was not in a position to defend its newly established frontiers with British Burma and French Indochina.

The high proportion of national minorities in Yunnan and Kwangsi posed a special problem for the imperial administration of China, for it needed to enhance its control without provoking anti-Chinese feeling. Many of the non-Han peoples of the frontier were only loosely administered by native chiefs, or *t'u-ssu*, a system which provided for local autonomy over

[28] The French sphere is described in Westel W. Willoughby, *Foreign Rights and Interests in China* (Baltimore, 1920), pp. 275–281.

[29] Pensri (Suvanij) Duke, *Les Relations entre la France et la Thailande (Siam) aux XIXème Siècle d'après les Archives des Affaires étrangères* (Bangkok, 1962); Sao Saimong Mangrai, "The Shan States and the British Annexation," Data Paper No. 57, Southeast Asia Program, Department of Asian Studies, Cornell University (Ithaca, 1965).

much of the upland areas of Szechwan, Kweichow, Yunnan, and Kwangsi. The term *t'u-ssu* denotes a variety of local officials confirmed in their positions by the government in Peking. There were different ranks of *t'u-ssu*, who might be either civil or military officials. During Ming and early Ch'ing times the various *t'u-ssu* positions were hereditary, but in the middle of the nineteenth century the Manchus adopted a policy of undermining the *t'u-ssu* and bringing their areas under direct administration. This policy, known as *kai-t'u kuei-liu*, was accompanied by an official scheme of Han colonization.[30]

The assimilationist policy of the Ch'ing dynasty was modified with respect to the *t'u-ssu* on the frontier of Yunnan by its desire to create a buffer against Anglo-French encroachment.

However, the *t'u-ssu* did not have the interests of China at heart. Far from maintaining the peace in the frontier area, they became the instigators of strife, and their capacity for protecting the frontier was negligible. They received no systematic instructions from the imperial government, and there was no examination of the character of their regimes such as existed with the Han Chinese civil servants. The result was that they were either seduced by external forces . . . or that they developed internal disorders. In the end, this method of operation brought the loss to China of the *t'u-ssu* domains of Meng-mi, Mu-pang, Meng-yang, Man-mu, and Meng-lang which became incorporated into British Burma. Additional losses involved Meng-so, Meng-la, Meng-wu, and Wu-te *t'u-ssu* domains which were annexed by the French in Indochina.[31]

In a formal sense, the abolition of all *t'u-ssu* in Kwangsi was complete by 1929 and in Yunnan by 1931, but some of the frontier *t'u-ssu* retained de facto control of their areas as late as the 1940s. A few of the more important *t'u-ssu* in Yunnan retained some influence even under the Communists.

The inclination of the frontier *t'u-ssu* to use British and French power for their own purposes was but one way in

[30] Chang Hsia-min, *Pien-chiang wen-t'i yü pien-chiang chien-she* (Frontier Questions and Frontier Development), (Taipei, 1958), pp. 68–70. Mathews, *Chinese-English Dictionary*, p. 479.
[31] Herold J. Wiens, *China's March Toward the Tropics*, p. 240.

which the non-Han peoples of Yunnan and Kwangsi expressed their dissatisfaction with the state of affairs under the waning Ch'ing dynasty. Considerable numbers of hill peoples turned to Christianity, while others migrated southward into Burma, Thailand, and Indochina. For instance, the Tibeto-Burman and Miao-Yao uplanders of Thailand are believed to have arrived in that country only within the past hundred years.[32] The uplanders of northern Indochina have been in their present habitat for perhaps one hundred fifty years.[33] A residual Chinese influence persists among the hill peoples who have migrated southward from China. Even at the turn of the century, Chinese was more of a lingua franca for the tribesmen of Burma than was Shan, the language of the lowlanders who dominate the area.[34] This remains true in northern Thailand today, where Chinese is more widely known among the hill people than is T'ai.[35]

Missionary activity was fairly intense among the hill peoples of Burma and Indochina during the colonial era, and many missionaries penetrated northward into the upland areas of south China. The Kwangsi and Yunnan hills were also entered by evangelists from missions situated in China. The lowlanders, both in China and in mainland Southeast Asia, were not generally susceptible to Christian proseletizing for they already adhered to Confucianism or Buddhism. Christianity was very attractive to the animistic hill peoples, however, for it made possible feelings of equality and self-respect which had been denied them by the arrogant plainsmen. These sentiments were reinforced by the loss of prestige, in the eyes of the hill peoples, of Chinese and Indian civilization by comparison with the modern civilization of the West. A similar development occurred in Assam, where numbers of Naga and other hill peoples, untouched by the Hinduism of the lowlanders,

[32] Gordon Young, *The Hill Tribes of Northern Thailand* (Bangkok, 1966).

[33] Henri Roux, "Quelques Minorités ethniques du Nord-Indochine," a special number of *France-Asie*, Nos. 92–93 (January–February 1954).

[34] J. George Scott and J. P. Hardiman, *Gazeteer of Upper Burma and the Shan States* (5 vols., Rangoon, 1900/1), 482.

[35] Personal observations made in January 1967.

were converted to Christianity. The success of the missionaries in Assam roused the jealousy of the Indian government, which finally ordered their expulsion. Much of the primary data on the hill peoples of China and adjacent states to the south was recorded by missionaries, an example of which is provided by the work of David C. Graham on the Miao of China.[36] Christian influence among the uplanders of Yunnan and Kwangsi persisted into the Communist period.

During the early phase of his revolutionary career, Sun Yat-sen used Hanoi as his headquarters in attempting to foment anti-Manchu uprisings in Yunnan and Kwangsi, but he does not seem to have been aware of the revolutionary potential of the minority peoples. When the Chinese revolution did succeed, in 1910/11, the Ch'ing dynasty was overthrown by revolutionaries established in the Yangtze valley. Thanks to physical remoteness and Anglo-French influence, Yunnan and Kwangsi were less affected by the turmoil of the early Republican and Warlord eras (1910–1916 and 1917–1927) than were most provinces of China. Military leaders in both provinces sought to extend their influence (that of Yunnan over Kweichow and Szechwan; that of Kwangsi over Kwangtung and Hunan) and to prevent the imposition of central-government control over them. The Kwangsi faction of the Kuomintang was at odds with the party leader, Chiang Kai-shek, following his assumption of dictatorial powers at the conclusion of the Northern Expedition (1926/7). This meant that the province enjoyed real autonomy. Nanking gained a degree of influence in Yunnan when its forces pursued the Communists into the province at the time of the Long March (1934/5), but its authority remained more nominal than real. Provincial leaders like Lung Yün (a Han-Yi half-caste) in Yunnan and Pai Chung-hsi (a Moslem) in Kwangsi enjoyed de facto independence. Their regional authority continued to be respected by the Nationalist government even during the Second World War, despite the influx of US military personnel and refugees from other parts of China.

[36] See the *Journal of the West China Border Research Society*, Vol. IX (1937).

During the first half of the twentieth century, Yunnan and Kwangsi stood aloof from the fundamental social changes effecting most parts of China. The student and labor movements scarcely penetrated these two provinces, which remained intensely conservative. Japanese forces entered Kwangsi and Yunnan only briefly during the Second World War. Enjoying quasi-independence, the provincial leaders in Kunming and Kweilin managed their affairs on the basis of self-interest and expediency. Although their areas of habitation were affected by economic changes, such as the development of commercial crops, the national minorities were, for the most part, ignored. When they posed a threat, however, they were ruthlessly crushed. This happened in the Pai-se region of Kwangsi when provincial forces destroyed a fledgling soviet area established among the Chuang in 1927.[37] In Yunnan, construction of the Burma road between Tali and the frontier, completed in 1938/9, was carried out mainly by corvée labor provided by the national minorities in the western part of the province. Large numbers of these workers perished.[38]

The formally proclaimed national minority policy of the Republican and Nationalist governments rationalized a policy of assimilation which the central government was only rarely able to implement. It masked the virtual independence of Tibet and Outer Mongolia by placing their affairs under a special bureau, resembling a Ch'ing administrative organ. Han settlement schemes were organized, usually by provincial or regional leaders, in the Sino-Mongol and Sino-Tibetan frontier zones, where new provinces were established (Jehol, Chahar, Suiyuan, Tsinghai, and Sikang). Minorities other than the Mongols and Tibetans, who were beyond the government's reach, were not accorded any special status. All citizens of China without regard to nationality were to be accorded equal rights, but since this Western idea conflicted with in-

[37] *Kuang-hsi ko-ming hui-i-lu* (Memoirs of the Revolution in Kwangsi), (Nanning, 1958).
[38] Chi Jen Chang, "The Minority Groups of Yunnan and Chinese Political Expansion into Southeast Asia," (unpublished Ph.D. dissertation, University of Michigan, 1956), p. 102.

herited Chinese values it was not generally adhered to. On the contrary, the traditional Han Chinese contempt for the national minorities was reinforced by Han Chinese nationalism, a completely new phenomenon. This nationalism, inspired by hatred of Manchu rule and by resistance to Western and Japanese imperialism, was extended in its application to all the non-Han peoples of China. It was the dominant theme of the Chinese revolution and provides one of the most striking elements of continuity between the thinking of Sun Yat-sen and that of Chiang Kai-shek.

2

THE IMPOSITION OF
COMMUNIST RULE

THE establishment of CCP control in south China proceeded from the cities to the countryside, reversing the
revolutionary process by which north China and Manchuria
had been won. The People's Liberation Army entered Kwangsi on November 7, 1949, and in a little over a month's time had
captured Kweilin, Liuchow, Nanning, and other key towns.
The Communists transferred the provincial capital from
Kweilin to Nanning, where a "people's government" for the
province was established on February 8, 1950. Kwangsi fell
within the jurisdiction of the South-central Military Government Council, a transitional administrative unit embracing
six provinces (Hunan, Hupeh, Kiangsi, Kwangtung, Kwangsi,
and Kweichow), with its seat at Hankow. With the exception
of Hainan Island, Kwangsi was the last area of this multi-
provincial unit to be won.[1]

The capture of Yunnan was peaceful in the sense that the

[1] *Hsin-hua yüeh-pao,* No. 5 (1950).

provincial governor, Lung Yün, declared himself in favor of the new regime before the arrival of the PLA in the province in December 1949, but the situation was not secure until March 1950. Among the Nationalist forces that had to be cleared from the province were Kwangsi units which had retired to the west before the advancing PLA. The new provincial authority was established at Kunming, the traditional capital of the province. Yunnan was placed under the authority of the Southwest Military Government Council, which, with its seat at Chungking, was responsible for Tibet, Sikang, and Szechwan, as well as Yunnan. With the exception of Tibet, Yunnan was the last area within this vast region to be won by the Communists.[2] Local guerrilla activity in support of the CCP's struggle for power in Kwangsi and Yunnan appears to have been limited to a popular force which developed in 1948 along the Yunnan-Kwangsi border between Kweichow and the Vietnamese frontier, an area inhabited mainly by national minority peoples.[3]

The Communist victory in Kwangsi and Yunnan caused the flight of approximately 15,000 Nationalist troops into Burma.[4] Considerable numbers of Nationalist troops also entered Indochina, but most of them were interned by the French authorities and eventually repatriated to Hainan and Taiwan. In Burma, however, the refugee soldiers formed an anti-Communist force that maintained itself on the mountainous Yunnanese frontier despite repeated efforts by the Burmese army to eject them. Called the "Li Mi Group" after its best known leader, General Li Mi, this force invaded Yunnan in July 1951 and briefly occupied the western part of the province before being thrown back by the PLA in August. Thereafter, General Li Mi retired to Taiwan while his army engaged in hit-and-run attacks against Yunnan from its base in Burma. Flights originating in Taiwan regularly brought supplies to the Li Mi Group, which was in contact with bands of Nationalist guer-

[2] *Jen-min jih-pao*, April 16, 1950.
[3] *Ibid.*
[4] *Kung-shang jih-pao*, January 3, 1951.

rillas stretching across Yunnan and Kwangsi all the way to the Kwangtung coast.[5]

The fact that Nationalist guerrillas in south China were in contact with the outside world added to the difficulties of the Communist authorities, who were struggling to pacify Yunnan and Kwangsi. Not only was liaison maintained between the guerrillas and the Li Mi Group, but the latter had the sympathy of the United States as well as Taiwan. The Peking *People's Daily* repeatedly charged the US with equipping, training, and supplying the remnant Nationalist forces in Burma.[6]

The anti-Communist guerrillas operating inside Yunnan and Kwangsi based themselves in remote hill areas, which tended to be the habitat of the non-Han Chinese. Their principal base was the K'awa (Wa) territory on the Sino-Burmese frontier. Good relations with the national minorities had not been a distinguishing feature of Kuomintang rule, but when necessity drove the Nationalists into the hills they quickly learned how to get along with the indigenous population. The presumed anti-Communist ardor of the national minorities became a fundamental tenet of the Nationalists. It was claimed that the non-Han peoples rallied to the support of the Li Mi Group when it entered Yunnan in 1951,[7] and cooperation with them remained an article of faith with Li Mi's followers thereafter.[8] By 1954, however, the Communists claimed that the implementation of the CCP's national minority policy in Yunnan had won the allegiance of the fraternal nationalities, who were said to be helping the PLA to suppress banditry in the frontier areas.[9]

The "liberation" of Kwangsi and Yunnan, then, meant no more than the seizure of the major towns and cities and con-

[5] *Nan-yang shang-pao*, December 2, 1952.

[6] See, for instance, *Jen-min jih-pao* for January 30, 1951, and February 13, 1952.

[7] *Hsing-tao jih-pao*, August 14, 1951.

[8] *T'ien-wen t'ai-pao*, November 14, 1952; *Chung-yang jih-pao*, December 6, 1953.

[9] *Nan-fang jih-pao*, September 9, 1954.

trol of the transportation system. The Communists found themselves somewhat in the position of an occupation force amidst a hostile population: what anti-Communist propaganda attributed to the PRC in general was actually true in parts of the south. The Cantonese-speaking Chinese were especially resistant to Communist rule, and the Cantonese-speaking area embraced southeastern Kwangsi as well as Kwangtung. As was noted in the previous chapter, Kweilin and its environs in northern Kwangsi comprise a Mandarin-speaking area, but the political localism of the people there was one of the factors which caused the new regime to move the capital to Nanning. Perhaps the most enthusiastic supporters of the Communists in Kwangsi were to be found among the Chuang people in the western part of the province, where a Soviet area, subsequently abandoned, had been established in 1927. The un-Sinicized Chuang of western Kwangsi had long been oppressed by the Han Chinese, and many of them welcomed the Communists.

In Yunnan, on the other hand, it was the national minorities who were most resistant to Communist rule, whereas the Han Chinese population of the province, which is Mandarin-speaking, generally accepted the new regime. The Han Chinese of Yunnan, unlike those of Kwangsi, retained a frontier tradition and looked to a strong central government for support against local threats to their security, such as might arise from antagonistic tribal peoples.

The main task of the new regime during its first years of control in Kwangsi and Yunnan was the "suppression of counterrevolutionaries." The Chairman of the Kwangsi people's government noted in a report of June 1950 that there were still 200,000 guns in the hands of the landlords and other evil people in the province. He said that many "bad elements" had joined the renegade KMT bandits, that the "feudal" attitude of Kwangsi-ism (*Kuang-hsi chu-i*) was widespread, and that the enemy was spreading rumors such as "the Americans have landed at Shanghai." There had been uprisings in several *hsien* in which a total of 150 pro-Communist activists had been

killed.[10] In May, the Chairman had declared that in the course
of pacification work during the five months since the take-over
of the province, 50,000 bandits had been wiped out.[11] This
figure rose to over 90,000 by the end of July, while the death
toll among Communist cadres and activists reached 500.[12] By
the autumn of 1950 the bandit problem had been basically
solved in areas where the Communist land program had been
implemented, but the mountainous areas of the province remained untouched. In these thinly inhabited areas, the provincial Vice-chairman noted, it was easy for bandits to operate.
In particular, there were three large areas which were still
seriously infected: the Yunnan-Kweichow-Hunan-Kwangsi
border region, the Ta-yao-shan range in the eastern part of the
province, and a strip of territory along the Sino-Vietnamese
border. With the support of "local feudal landlords," the bandits in these areas were said to be wrecking communications
and spreading disorder.[13] It is likely that these landlords in the
frontier districts who were so staunchly anti-Communist had
a high proportion of non-Han-Chinese tenants. Within a period of two years following the establishment of Communist
power in Kwangsi, 470,000 bandits were reported to have been
killed and 440,000 captured in the province. Nevertheless, the
us-backed KMT reactionaries were still considered a threat, and
it was noted that Kwangsi, like Yunnan, was still infected by
the attitude of "worship America, fear America."[14]

In Yunnan, the "counter-revolutionaries" were most active
in the mountains along the frontier, according to Teng Hsiao-
p'ing, Chairman of the Southwest Military Government Coun-

[10] "June 28, 1950, Half-year Work Report of the Kwangsi Provincial
People's Government," published in *Hsing-tao jih-pao*, August 6, 1950.

[11] "1950 Work Tasks of the Kwangsi Provincial People's Government," *Kuang-hsi jih-pao*, May 14, 1950.

[12] The Vice-Chairman's "September 19, 1950, Work Report of the
Kwangsi Provincial People's Government," *Chang-chiang jih-pao*, September 25, 1950.

[13] *Ibid.*

[14] Report by the Vice-Chairman of the South-central Military Government Committee, in *Jen-min jih-pao*, November 1, 1951.

cil.[15] Even two years after the formal Communist victory in the province, it was admitted that the frontier areas were still bandit-infested.[16] The security situation in Yunnan was complicated by the fact that the bandits operated in national minority regions. As late as 1955, an observer of the Yunnan scene said that

> The evil doings of the enemy in the frontier national minority regions become more and more manifest. They brazenly plunder, kill, and create rumors; they scheme to spoil nationality relations and create nationality divisions, and to wreck the national defense of the motherland.[17]

Pacification was followed and sometimes accompanied by a number of other programs which, like pacification itself, proceeded from the towns to the countryside. The most important of these was land reform. The first step in the agrarian program was the reduction of taxes and rent, announced by the Communists from their position in the cities.[18] In the spring of 1951, a three-stage scheme for carrying out land reform had been devised for the southwest region, but the national minority areas were specifically excluded.[19] By July 1952 the second stage had penetrated most of Yunnan's sixty-six *hsien* and affected about half the population of the province.[20] Disaster relief, which could also be made to serve political ends, took precedence over land reform in Kwangsi, struck in 1949/50 by floods and drought which affected twenty percent of the population.[21]

It was observed that the land reform program, as it developed, directly served the task of bandit-suppression in Kwangsi.[22] Although land reform was held up in Kwangsi be-

[15] *Hsin-hua yüeh-pao*, October 1950.

[16] Progress reports on Yunnan presented to the Southwest Military Government Council, in *Ta-kung-pao*, November 24, 1951.

[17] *Ta-kung-pao*, August 1, 1955.

[18] "Situation report on work in the Southwest," *Hsin-hua yüeh-pao*, May 1950.

[19] *Jen-min jih-pao*, October 31, 1951.

[20] *Hsin-hua jih-pao*, September 29, 1952.

[21] *Hsing-tao jih-pao*, June 28, 1950.

[22] *Chang-chiang jih-pao*, September 25, 1950.

cause of the difficulties encountered in pacification,[23] by June
1951 it was said that sixty-five percent of the population of the
province had experienced the land-reform movement.[24] Here,
as in Yunnan and elsewhere, the national minorities were excluded from the scope of the Land Reform Law of June 30,
1950. Progress in setting up "all-circles representative congresses," the political accompaniment of land reform, was in-
dicative of the general security situation. As of September
1950, such congresses had still not been convened in twenty-
eight of the nearly seventy *hsien* in Kwangsi.[25] The patriotic
movement called "Resist America, aid Korea" was another important vehicle for the institution of government control: as of
the autumn of 1951 it had reached ninety percent of the urban
and fifty percent of the rural population in Kwangsi,[26] while in
Yunnan the corresponding figures were eighty percent and
sixty percent.[27] Inasmuch as this movement was first "launched
in the cities" and then "spread to the peasant villages and distant frontier regions," few national minority regions could
have been affected by it, although it was intended that the
non-Han Chinese should be included.

Just as the countryside lagged behind the towns with respect
to the implementation of basic Communist programs in
Kwangsi and Yunnan, so these provinces lagged behind by
comparison with other provinces in their respective regions.

The beginnings of national minority work

Prior to the promulgation in August 1952 of the *General
Program for Regional Autonomy*, local authorities who dealt
with non-Han peoples in Yunnan and Kwangsi were guided by
the broad provisions of the 1949 Common Program (see also
the Introduction, above). The intent of the Common Program
with respect to the national minority regions was to restore the
unity between the Han and non-Han peoples which, accord-

---

[23] *Hsin-hua yüeh-pao*, April 1950.
[24] *Nan-fang jih-pao*, September 5, 1952.
[25] *Chang-chiang jih-pao*, September 25, 1950.
[26] *Chang-k'ou jih-pao*, November 28, 1951.
[27] *Jen-min jih-pao*, October 31, 1951.

ing to the official version, had been rent by the *ancien regime*.[28] Nationalities unity was to serve the cause of anti-imperialism, and was to be furthered by equality and mutual aid among all the country's national groups. During the period of the *Common Program*, therefore, policies which might produce tension and animosity were to be deferred. One of these was land reform. In other respects, however, the national minorities were to be accorded the same treatment as the Han Chinese.

Chang Yün-i, Chairman of the Kwangsi Provincial People's Government Council, issued instructions on May 12, 1950, to the effect that the national minorities should be included in the famine relief work then being carried out in the province and that they should participate in the "all-circles people's representative congresses" being established as interim political organs. He also said that national-minority cadres, along with peasant and proletarian cadres, must be speedily trained.[29] According to Lin Piao, Chairman of the South-central Military Government Council, national minorities could also be included in land reform, provided that special attention was paid to conditions in their areas. Communities which were heavily dependent on remittances from overseas Chinese were frequently lumped together with the national minorities as requiring special treatment.[30]

The Chairman of the Southwest Military Government Council, Teng Hsiao-p'ing, observed with satisfaction in the autumn of 1950 that no rebellions involving national minorities had occurred. Many problems remained, however. He looked forward to the implementation of the Party's program of regional autonomy for nationalities and to the resolution of their problems in the economic, health, and education fields.[31] A contemporary report on the national minority situation in the southwest made note of the need to oppose great-nation chauvinism on the part of the Han Chinese and narrow nation-

[28] See, for instance, T'ang Chen-tsung, *Chung-kuo shao-shu min-tsu ti hsin mien-mao* (The new appearance of China's national minorities), (Peking, 1953).

[29] *Hsin-hua yüeh-pao*, June 1950.

[30] *Chang-chiang jih-pao*, February 16, 1950.

[31] *Hsin-hua yüeh-pao*, October 1950.

alism on the part of the minorities. The greater unity of all the
nationalities which would thus be created would help to "establish the nation's defense, clean out bandits, and build a new
southwest." When reforms were introduced into the national-
minority areas, they would have to meet the special needs of
the local people. For this work, large numbers of national-
minority cadres would be needed; their training would be the
responsibility of the people's government. The report promised that questions affecting the national minorities would be
dealt with in accordance with the provisions of the *Common
Program*.[32]

During 1950 and 1951 the Central People's Government
(CPG) despatched teams to all national-minority regions to convey Peking's solicitude for the fraternal nationalities and to
report back on conditions there. Kwangsi was visited by a
team, led by Li Te-chuan, which was assigned to the south-
central region, while Yunnan was visited by the southwest
team under the leadership of Liu Ko-p'ing. In her report,[33]
Chairman Li drew attention to an important contradiction
confronting implementation of the CCP's national minority
policy when she observed that many of the Chuang people in
Kwangsi were not willing to be identified as Chuang but pre-
ferred to pass as Han people. This was a problem which was
not confined to the Chuang. It was true of all the lowland-
dwelling national-minority peoples who had been extensively
Sinicized. Li Te-chuan also observed that, quite apart from
any unwillingness to be identified as non-Han peoples, some
of the national minorities had adopted Han Chinese ways to
such an extent as to be indistinguishable as separate groups.
She said that in the south-central region generally, good progress was being made with such movements as bandit suppression, the convening of popular assemblies, the training of
national minority cadres, preparatory work for the implementation of regional autonomy, and the sending of mobile health
teams into remote hill areas. Li Te-chuan noted that the ideo-

[32] *Hsin-hua yüeh-pao*, September 1950.
[33] *Jen-min jih-pao*, December 23, 1951. The report was delivered on
November 16 to the Government Affairs Council.

logical training of some Han cadres responsible for national minority affairs was inadequate, and she emphasized the importance of developing trade and communications.

In his report on the southwest,[34] Liu Ko-p'ing commented on the CCP's policy of bestowing formal political rights on the national minorities. Among local government organs which met the requirements of this policy, he mentioned the "democratic nationality coalition government" of the county of Kunming, capital of Yunnan. He expressed the opinion that the exercise of political rights on the part of the national minorities served to heighten their self-consciousness. Referring to the problem of trade and communicatons, he mentioned the fact that it still took a month to travel from Kunming to the southwest Yunnan border, a distance of about five hundred miles by way of the old Burma Road. A noteworthy feature of the southwest with respect to the problem of education among the national minorities was the existence of numerous schools established by foreign missionaries. Coming to the problem of national defense, Liu observed that the long frontier in the southwest was inhabited entirely by national minority peoples, some of whom lived on both sides of the frontier. For instance, the Karen people of Burma extended into the Paoshan area of Yunnan, making for easy trans-frontier communications. This situation was made even more vexatious when the people in question were Christians, as was the case with the Nu people in Pi-chiang *hsien*, in the Salween Valley. In this area, the CPG's national-minorities inspection team even met local Christians who had the effrontery to declare that they had been doing national minority work for several decades! As Chairman Liu noted, it was precisely in this region of western Yunnan that the remnant Nationalist forces, or Li Mi Group, was most active.

The visits of the CPG teams to Yunnan and Kwangsi punctuated the early efforts of the local authorities to develop national minority work in these two provinces. Pacification was the most pressing item on their agenda. The hills of Kwangsi

[34] *Yün-nan jih-pao*, July 24, 1951. The report was presented to the Government Affairs Council on May 11.

and Yunnan, thinly inhabited by non-Han peoples, were in-
fested with anti-Communist forces, or "bandits." For instance,
the national minority people in Kwangsi's Lung-lin *hsien*,
adjacent to Vietnam, had admittedly been influenced by the
bandits because they at first had not believed that the PRC
would be able to protect them. However, we are told that
Communist cadres patiently won over the people and developed a local militia which finally surrounded and destroyed
the bandits.[35] In southern Yunnan, where neither "American
imperialism" nor the "Chiang Kai-shek remnant gang" were
reconciled to their defeat, the national minority peoples experienced the depradations of the Yunnan Anti-Communist
National Salvation Army which operated from Burma. However, confidence was gradually being restored among the local
people, thanks in part to the energetic implementation of the
movement for the suppression of counter-revolutionaries.[36]
The task of pacification was also furthered by the "Resist
America, aid Korea" movement, one of the few country-wide
movements that was vigorously applied in the national minority areas during the early years of the regime. It was reported to have helped develop a patriotic spirit among the
non-Han frontier peoples. When the "Resist America, aid Korea" movement reached the township of An-t'ai in Lo-ch'eng
hsien of Kwangsi in September 1951, the national minority
peoples there enthusiastically contributed to the national effort 1,559 pine logs which they had planted and felled themselves.[37] In Yunnan, the Miao and Pu-lang people of Meng-tzu
hsien responded to the movement by establishing a self-defense
force which stood guard day and night, thus putting an end to
banditry in the area.[38] In the *hsien* seat of Ch'e-li in southern
Yunnan, more than 120 representatives of various circles and
nationalities held a "Resist America, aid Korea" meeting at
which they pledged themselves to "enhance nationalities

[35] *Kuang-hsi jih-pao*, December 6, 1951. Lung-lin *hsien* attained some
notoriety by virtue of its having been visited by the CPG inspection team.
[36] *Yün-nan jih-pao*, September 26, 1951. "Counter-revolutionaries" is
the term used to describe anti-Communists lurking among "the people."
[37] *Kuang-hsi jih-pao*, March 4, 1952.
[38] *Yün-nan jih-pao*, September 25, 1951.

unity, maintain the country's defenses, expand trade and production, and pay their taxes."[39]

The first impression the national minority peoples of Yunnan and Kwangsi had of the PRC was usually conveyed by the PLA. The PLA had achieved fame throughout China for its decent treatment of the common people. Further indoctrination was given troops assigned to national minority areas. They were told that it was essential that special care be taken to ensure that the sensibilities of the national minority peoples should not be offended. "While hunting down rebels," the Deputy First Secretary of the Kwangsi provincial CCP bureau declared, "Army regulations make it mandatory that the correct policy of the central authorities concerning respect for the customs and habits of the national minorities be carried out." He went on to say that designated units should engage in propaganda activities and take part in the relief work being initiated by the government. Such efforts, he observed, had already been rewarded, with national minority peoples in different areas giving active support to the PLA in its bandit-suppression work.[40] The PLA had a similar role in Yunnan.[41] PLA activities in support of the common people, and the frontier peoples in particular, were often romanticized in stories for popular consumption.[42]

The sequel to pacification was the carrying out of the Common Program's promise of full political rights for the national minorities. Because pacification was itself a slow and difficult process, the organs of political power that were initially established in national minority areas took a variety of forms; only after promulgation of the General Program for Regional Autonomy in August 1952 was this political structure systematized. The first national minority peoples to be politically organized were those living mixed with, or in close proximity to, Han Chinese communities. Where their numbers were

[39] Yün-nan jih-pao, December 5, 1951.

[40] Kuang-hsi jih-pao, December 21, 1951.

[41] Hsin-hua yüeh-pao, May 1950.

[42] See, for instance, Chu-shou pien-chiang ti wei-kuo chan-shih (The nation's defenders stationed on the frontiers), (Peking, 1953).

few, they simply sent representatives to a predominantly Han-Chinese political institution. The principal institutions in Han Chinese areas usually took the form of "peasant congresses" in rural areas or, in urban areas, "all-circles congresses." Where they were more numerous, the national minorities established "all-nationalities congresses" which frequently included Han Chinese. Given the jumbled pattern of settlement of the various nationalities—Han and non-Han—in Yunnan and Kwangsi, it was inevitable that expediency should take precedence over consistency in the formation of these institutions. Such associations were supposed to be organized in every *hsien* and city, and their chief function was to popularize government regulations.[43]

The policy of regional autonomy applied more particularly to national minorities that comprised distinct and separate communities. Governments based on the principle of regional autonomy were established for minority communities which constituted major concentrations of population or which occupied large areas. A variant type of administrative unit was the coalition government, established when two or more fairly large national minority groups shared a single, cohesive area. Put crudely, regional autonomy was to be exercised by national minorities which constituted half or more of the population of the area in which they were found, while coalition governments were to be established for national minorities representing one-third to one-half the population of their areas; the democratic rights of national minorities comprising less than one-third of the population were to be assured merely by guaranteeing adequate representation in the local organ of administration.[44] Such organs of political power were being set up well before the formal promulgation of the *General Program*. Table 1 indicates the number of each type in Yunnan as of November 1951.[45]

An example of a national minority area which put regional autonomy into practice at an early date was Hsin-meng town-

[43] *Hsin-hua yüeh-pao*, No. 5 (1950).
[44] *Chang-chiang jih-pao*, November 26, 1951.
[45] *Ta-kung-pao* (Chungking), November 24, 1951.

TABLE 1

	Autonomous Region Governments	Democratic Coalition Governments
Special Administrative Areas		4
Hsien (county)	4	13
Ch'ü (district)	2	11
Hsiang (township)	24	5

ship of Ho-shi *hsien*, south of Kunming. Under the leadership of the Yunnan provincial people's government, the various "fraternal nationalities" in this area were reported to have established the "Hsin-meng nationalities coalition government" on September 10, 1951. The Chairman of the new government resolved at its opening meeting that under the leadership of the CCP and Chairman Mao the people would strive to remould themselves and to increase production.[46] Another example of an early autonomous region was the "Lisu people's autonomous *hsien*" established in the northern reaches of the Salween Valley in Yunnan in September 1951. This autonomous *hsien* was formally established at an "all-nationalities, all-circles, people's representative meeting." After the meeting, the representatives were reported to have written to Chairman Mao as follows:

> We, people of various nationalities, must in the future strengthen unity, strenuously resist any new activities on the part of imperialism, and strengthen the frontiers of the motherland.[47]

In Kwangsi, a "nationalities democratic coalition government" was established in July 1951 for the various nationalities living in Lung-sheng *hsien*, a part of Kweilin special district. This was the first administrative unit based on the principle of regional autonomy to be established in the province. In Lung-sheng, the CCP was able to draw on the services

---

[46] *Yün-nan jih-pao*, September 25, 1951.
[47] *Yün-nan jih-pao*, December 18, 1951.

of veteran Communists who had served the Party as guerrilla leaders in the struggle against the Nationalists.[48]

The establishment of autonomous and coalition governments for the national minorities in Kwangsi and Yunnan was generally based on the principle of the united front: that is, the CCP entrusted "upper-level personages," who enjoyed "close connections with the masses," with the task of heading the new administration. The fact that such a leader had remained in China rather than fleeing across the frontier was probably sufficient recommendation in most cases,[49] and many of the new administrative areas established for the nationalities revealed a close correspondence with the old *t'u-ssu* domains. The Tibetan autonomous region in Sikang province, established during the visit there of the CPG inspection team, was evidently considered a model for the new administrative system for national minorities. By early 1952 the provincial authorities in Yunnan and Kwangsi had gained considerable experience in national minority work. In reports delivered to the second (enlarged) session of the CPG's Nationalities Affairs Commission in February, Chang Chih-i and Wang Wei-chou, the Commissioners for Nationality Affairs in the south-central and southwest regions, respectively, left no doubt that in their view the policy of regional autonomy for national minorities could be successfully implemented in Kwangsi and Yunnan. At the same time, however, they made it clear that the influence of the new regime was only just beginning to penetrate the more remote national minority areas, that serious errors and shortcomings had occurred in the work of the cadres assigned to nationalities affairs, and that further difficulties could be anticipated.[50]

[48] *Nan-fang jih-pao*, December 28, 1951.

[49] Sometimes the son of a chief would flee, and the father remained, or vice-versa, so that in any eventuality their claim to local leadership would be maintained. Inevitably, the individual who fled was associated with local Kuomintang leaders. Tribal leaders used by the Communists frequently received none-too-rigorous ideological training in Peking. This information is based on personal interviews held in North Thailand in January 1967.

[50] Chang's report was carried in the *Jen-min jih-pao*, February 18, 1952, and Wang's in the *Hsin-hua jih-pao*, February 24, 1952.

3

THE ESTABLISHMENT
OF AUTONOMOUS
AREAS: PHASE ONE

THE establishment of autonomous areas for the national minorities in Yunnan and Kwangsi was greatly accelerated by the promulgation of the *General Program for the Implementation of Regional Autonomy (Chung-kuo jen-min kung-ho-kuo min-tsu ch'ü-yü tzu-ch'ih shih-shih kang-yao)*, previously discussed in the Introduction. The *General Program* was approved by the Central People's Government Council at its eighteenth meeting, held on August 9, 1952. At the same time, regulations were adopted concerning the establishment of democratic coalition governments for areas inhabited by different nationalities and the protection of the democratic rights of dispersed nationalities. These laws were based on the *Common Program* and three years' experience in nationalities work. The Party's program was hailed as the application by Mao Tse-tung of Marxist-Leninist theory to the resolution of the national question in China.

Only the large autonomous areas of Yunnan established during the early post-1949 years became permanent features of the administrative map of China. The units comprising individual *hsiang* and *ch'ü* were discarded or amalgamated into larger units, whereas the autonomous areas comprising one or more *hsien* generally remained. This process of consolidation worked against the Marxist-Leninist ideal of self-rule for national minorities because it meant the loss of regional autonomy for small and scattered groupings of non-Han peoples. Administrative convenience was no doubt one reason for the discontinuation of sub-*hsien*-sized autonomous areas. A more important reason may have been the adoption of the *hsien* as the basic unit for the development of the country. Only the *hsien* contained an administrative seat with a concentration, however small, of Han Chinese, the only reliable foundation for political control of the south China frontier regions. The development of *hsien* units under Han Chinese domination had also been the pattern of Kuomintang rule in the minority areas of the south.

In general, the autonomous *hsien* and autonomous *chou* (perfectures) established in Yunnan during the 1950s have persisted down to the present. They were not established in random order; rather, the frontier areas received priority over interior regions of national minority habitation. Some order of priorities had to be established, since the resources at the disposal of the province for carrying out national minority work were limited. By the end of 1954, the task of organizing autonomous areas along the frontier had been accomplished, whereas the major autonomous units in the interior were established during the years 1956–1958. The frontier areas of Yunnan will be discussed in this chapter and the interior areas in the next. The 1954 dividing line corresponds to the adoption of the state constitution and the CCP's shift to the "general line for the transition period" (transition to socialism) as its guide to action.[1]

The relatively simple ethnic make-up of Kwangsi, as compared with Yunnan, enabled the provincial authorities there

[1] The evolving ideological framework of Chinese Communism is discussed in Peter S. H. Tang, *Communist China Today* (Washington, 1961), Vol. I.

to complete the main task of establishing autonomous areas during the two-year period 1952/53. As will be seen, the creation of the provincial-level Kwangsi Chuang Autonomous Region in 1958, involving an elevation and expansion of the West Kwangsi Chuang Autonomous *Chou*, took place outside the existing framework for the establishment of autonomous areas for national minorities and will be considered in the next chapter.

The West Kwangsi Chuang autonomous area
(*Kuei-hsi chuang-tsu tzu-ch'ih ch'ü*)

Quite elaborate preparations were made for the establishment of the West Kwangsi Chuang autonomous area (WKC), which came into being in December 1952. A Preparatory Committee was set up in October, following an important nationalities work conference for Kwangsi held the previous month. The composition of the committee reflected the ethnic composition of the area of western Kwangsi in which the Chuang people were to exercise autonomy. Of a total membership of twenty-eight, there were fifteen Chuang, seven Han, two Yao, two Miao, and two T'ung members. The Chairman and one of the two Vice-chairmen were Chuang, but the other vice-chairman was a Han Chinese named Chao Cho-yün. Chao, whose regular job was Chairman of the CCP's United Front Department for Kwangsi province, probably played the key role on the Committee. At what was apparently its first meeting, held on October 6 and 7, the Committee was addressed by Liu Ko-p'ing, Vice-commissioner of the CPG's Nationalities Affairs Commission, and Chang Chih-i, Commissioner of a similar body within the Central-south Military Government Council. Liu declared that the Chuang people must definitely be considered as a "nation" and that they would certainly prosper after the achievement of regional autonomy. Liu transmitted a report on nationalities work from Commissioner Li Wei-han and expressed four wishes concerning the creation of an autonomous area for the Chuang. He hoped: first, that Han cadres and people would aid their Chuang comrades in establishing the autonomous area; second, that the Chuang comrades would unite with and learn from the Han people; third, that the Chuang comrades would assist other nationalities within the autonomous area; and, fourth, that all cadres would strengthen their understanding of nationalities policy and energetically carry out mass propaganda. Chang Chih-i, in his address, warned against great-nation chauvinism, which posed a real danger to the successful implementation of regional autonomy. He noted that great-nation chauvinism might manifest itself not only among Han people vis-à-vis minorities like the Chuang but also among Chuang people vis-à-vis smaller nationalities, sub-minorities like the Yao.[2]

At a subsequent meeting, held on October 31, the Preparatory Committee discussed the question of why the Chuang people should be considered a nation and how they would benefit by the establishment of an autonomous area. The meeting was attended by Chuang cadres and Chuang students as well as by members of the Committee. The principal address at the meeting was made by the Committee's Chuang Vice-chairman, Hsieh Hou-ch'ou. He enumerated the Stalinist criteria for a "nation" and argued that these were fully met by the Chuang people. Responding to evident skepticism about the need to establish a Chuang autonomous area, he said that the Chuang masses would more enthusiastically commit themselves to the task of attaining socialism if their own affairs were managed by representatives of their own people, by men who spoke the Chuang language. Scolding critics of the Party's national-minority policy, he observed that advocacy of an assimilationist policy, alleged to have been favored by the Kuomintang, was counter-revolutionary. He admitted, however, that the Chuang people, being almost exclusively farmers with no interest in commerce, relied on the many Han tradesmen who lived in their area; nor did he deny that, at least in commercial relations, Chinese was the lingua franca in the Chuang area as well as elsewhere in the province.[3]

Vice-chairman Hsieh's argument in favor of "nation" status for the Chuang people of Kwangsi paralleled that made a few

[2] *Kuang-hsi jih-pao*, November 8, 1952.
[3] *Ibid.*

days earlier in a feature article in the *Kwangsi Daily*.[4] According to this article, the Chuang people fully possessed all four of the characteristics of a nation as defined by Stalin: community of language, territory, economic life, and culture. With a population of more than 5.4 million concentrated in the area of the Tso and Yu Rivers in northwest Kwangsi, the Chuang people had a history going back several millenia. They possessed a uniform system of agriculture based on the flooded-field method and use of the plow.

Writing in the same issue of the *Kwangsi Daily*, a Chuang student recalled that when he first arrived at the Nationalities Institute in Nanning he was asked his nationality and he replied, "Han." His questioner then asked, "What language do you speak at home?" "Chuang," said the student. "Chuang speakers are Chuang people, not Han," said the other. At first the student did not accept this, and for a long time was careful not to talk to any other Chuang. Later on a Yao student inquired about his nationality, and he replied, "Han." Then the Yao student asked him what he spoke at home. Not knowing how to reply, he said nothing. "Ah, then you are Chuang," the Yao student said. The student was finally relieved of his anxieties when, after studying the ideas of Mao and Stalin on the national question, he realized that Chuang nationality was nothing to be ashamed of and that his feelings of inferiority had been caused by the "great Han chauvinism" of the old Kuomintang regime. He realized that the Chuang people were politically, economically, and culturally less advanced than the Han people, but expected that this backwardness would speedily be overcome following the establishment of the WKC.[5]

Statistics published a few weeks prior to the formal establishment of the WKC revealed that the new administrative area would comprise 34 *hsien* with a total area of 111,695 square

[4] Chang Ching-ning, "Kuang-hsi chuang-tsu ti chien-tan chieh-shao" (A brief introduction to the Chuang people of Kwangsi), *Ibid.*, November 5, 1952.

[5] Su Yüan-min, "Wo je-ai tzu-chi ti min-tsu" (I love my own nationality), *Ibid.*

kilometers and a population of 6,268,935. The population consisted of:

Han	22 percent
Chuang	67 percent
Other nationalities	11 percent

Cadres from each of the constituent *hsien* attended an enlarged meeting of the Preparatory Committee on November 6, after which they returned to their respective *hsien* to carry out intensive propaganda on behalf of the new autonomous area. The next step was for each *hsien* to convene an "all-nationalities, all-circles, people's representative congress" (*ko-tsu ko-chieh jen-min tai-piao hui-i*), whose participants were to be imbued with the spirit of the earlier meeting of the Preparatory Committee as well as with the ideology of regional autonomy for nationalities. The main task of these *hsien* congresses was to select delegates to the first session of the "all-nationalities, all-circles, people's representative congress" for the WKC, which was convened in Nanning on December 6. Following the conclusion of the *hsien* congresses, the participants were to spread out into the villages to carry out propaganda and organization work at the mass level.[6] During this phase of concerted effort, the Preparatory Committee was aided by the central, regional, and provincial governments.[7]

Precise regulations for the make-up of the area-wide people's congress were published by the Preparatory Committee in mid-November.[8] In addition to delegates representing the various nationalities, the CCP, government, PLA, and mass organizations were also to be represented. There were also to be specially invited delegates. Delegates from the nationalities were to be chosen on a proportional basis; however, this principle could be stretched to the advantage of small and scattered national groups to insure that they were adequately represented. All levels of and circles within each nationality,

[6] *Ibid.*, November 16, 1952.
[7] *Ibid.*, December 3, 1952.
[8] *Ibid.*, November 16, 1952.

including religious personages, spokesmen for farmers, nationality cadres, traditional leaders, and women's groups, were to be represented. For the Han and Chuang nationality, there would be delegates representing the interests of businessmen and workers, as well. In detail, the representatives were to be distributed as follows:

A. Nationality representatives:

Chuang	445
Yao	74
Miao	21
T'ung	17
other nationalities	17
Sub-total	656

B. CCP, government, PLA, mass organizations:

CCP	20
government	40
PLA	20
mass organizations	12
Sub-total	92

C. Specially invited guests: 30

Grand Total   778

The territorial distribution of the delegates was as follows:

A. From the 34 *hsien* being incorporated:

Yung-ning district	(11 *hsien*)	280
I-shan district	(10 *hsien*)	217
Pai-se district	(12 *hsien*)	238
Ch'in-chou district	(1 *hsien*)	10
Sub-total		745

B. From elsewhere in province: 33

Grand Total   778

In addition, the congress was to be attended by one hundred observers from various places in the country.[9]

The congress met in Nanning from December 6 to 9, inclusive. Prior to the opening of the congress, the delegates attended a three-day course at the Nationalities Institute

9 *Ibid.*

ADMINISTRATIVE DIVISIONS OF KWANGSI IN 1955
(Exclusive of Autonomous Hsien)

The names on the map are those of special districts.

The West Kwangsi Chuang Autonomous Area occupies
all of the province west of the heavy line.

*Chin-chow was long a part of neighboring
Kwangtung Province.

(Min-tsu hsüeh-yüan) in Nanning during which they pon-
dered the question of why it was necessary for an autonomous
area to be established for the Chuang people in western
Kwangsi and considered the various tasks which lay ahead for
the new administrative unit. As outlined in the opening address delivered by the Chuang chairman of the Preparatory
Committee, T'an Ying-chi, the tasks of the congress were: to
discuss and approve the organization of the people's government for the WKC autonomous area; to elect a government
council as well as a chairman and vice-chairman of the government; to formally establish the new administration (people's
government council); and to discuss future tasks. Liu Ko-
p'ing, from Peking, and Chang Chih-i, from Wuhan, were

again on hand. Congratulatory telegrams were received from the south-central regional government and party organizations. This fanfare emphasized the exceptional position of the WKC autonomous area, which not only had the largest minority-group population of any autonomous area in the country but which was also administratively unique, being equivalent to about half a province. Like other autonomous areas, however, its administrative functions were to be exercised as a local organ of state power, in accordance with the *General Program*.[10] In a telegraphed greeting to the central authorities, the delegates announced the victorious conclusion of the congress, which had brought into being the People's Government of the WKC autonomous area. The telegram stated, "We national minorities are well aware that imperialism is our cruelest enemy, and that your difficult war in Korea, which is smashing American imperialism, has made possible the establishment of the Chuang people's autonomous area."[11] The date of the formal establishment of the autonomous area was December 9, and Nanning, also the provincial capital, became the administrative seat. On the following day, 50,000 people participated in festivities in Nanning marking the establishment of the autonomous area.[12]

The establishment of the WKC autonomous area was an extraordinary event. To a certain extent, it took place outside the framework in which other autonomous areas in Kwangsi were created. During the first year of national minority work in the province, which began in July 1951 under the stimulus of the visit to the province of the CPG's inspection team and ended with the September 1952 Kwangsi nationalities work conference,[13] there was no suggestion that a large autonomous area for the Chuang people would be established. Indeed, there is considerable evidence that the Chuang were not then

---

[10] *Jen-min jih-pao*, December 8, 1952.

[11] *Ibid.*, December 12, 1952.

[12] *Ta-kung jih-pao* (Hong Kong), December 18, 1952.

[13] This periodization is suggested by Chao Cho-yün, "Kuang-hsi shen shao-shu min-tsu ti-ch'ü ti hsin mien-mao" (The new appearance of the national minority areas in Kwangsi province), *Jen-min jih-pao*, April 6, 1954.

considered to be a national minority at all, and that it was only at the September work conference that a decision to this effect was made. During the first year of national minority work in Kwangsi, the Chuang people were not usually dealt with in discussions of national minority questions; when, after September 1952, they were included, an evident lack of statistics often made it necessary to exclude them from existing enumerations. For instance, in an article published on October 1, 1952, the deputy head of the National Minority Affairs Commission of the Kwangsi Provincial People's Government says, "there are altogether four thousand national minority cadres in the whole province (not including cadres of Chuang nationality)," and again, "in the past two years and more, the number of national minority representatives [in the *hsien*-level people's congresses] totals 542 (not including areas of the Chuang nationality)."[14] The WKC autonomous area made its appearance barely two months after its inception at the September conference, and officials from outside the province seem to have interferred to an unusual degree in the course of its establishment. In fact, there is some reason to think that the Chuang area was created by the CCP Central Committee for reasons of domestic politics and that its chosen instrument was the south-central regional bureau of the United Front Work Department at Wuhan.

OTHER AUTONOMOUS AREAS IN KWANGSI

While the West Kwangsi Chuang autonomous area was being established in December 1952, other autonomous areas in Kwangsi had already been set up or were in the process of formation. The Lung-sheng Multinational autonomous area came into existence in August 1951. The Ta-yao-shan [Great Yao Mountain] Yao nationality autonomous area, established in May 1952, was next. The San-chiang T'ung nationality autonomous area came into existence before the end of the year, followed in 1953 by the Ta-miao-shan [Great Miao Mountain]

[14] Ch'en An, "Liang nien to lai kuang-hsi shao-shu min-tsu kung-tso ti ch'eng-chiu" (Accomplishments in national minority work in Kwangsi during the past two years), *Kuang-hsi jih-pao*, October 1, 1952.

Miao nationality autonomous area and the Lung-lin Multinational autonomous area. The establishment of these five areas, all of which were later to be redesignated "*hsien*," was interpreted as basically meeting Kwangsi's requirements with reference to implementing the policy of regional autonomy for national minorities.[15] Lung-lin is located in the extreme western portion of the province, adjacent to Yunnan, while the Ta-yao-shan is situated in the east-central portion of the province; the other three—Ta-miao-shan, San-chiang, and Lung-sheng—are strung along the northern fringe of Kwangsi, adjacent to Kweichow or Hunan. It only remained, several years later, to establish two other Yao autonomous *hsien* (Pa-ma and Tu-an) in the central portion of the province. In the extreme southeast, on the Gulf of Tongking, a coalition government for the Yao and P'ien uplanders of the Shih-wan-shan area was established in October 1952. Prior to 1965, this region was under the administration of Kwangtung province. During that time the autonomous area in the Shih-wan-shan area became known as Tung-hsing Multinational autonomous *hsien*, while a Chuang nationality autonomous *hsien* was set up immediately to the north, at Ch'in-pei.

Small autonomous areas which had but an ephemeral existence cannot be considered here. National minority *hsiang*, of which there were forty in Kwangsi in October 1953,[16] were either absorbed into larger units or abolished; similarly, national minority districts (*ch'ü*), of which there were twelve in October 1954,[17] were either transformed into *hsien* or abolished. With concentrated groups of non-Han-Chinese peoples occurring in all but twelve of Kwangsi's seventy-four *hsien* and all but one of its five cities, the principle of regional autonomy for national minorities could not be carried out to perfection. Compromise was necessary. According to Chao Cho-yün, 5.8 million of the province's 6.3 million national minorities lived within the various autonomous areas which existed in the spring of 1954: one circuit (*shu*), five *hsien*, eight districts

[15] Ch'en An, *op. cit.*
[16] *Kuang-hsi jih-pao*, October 16, 1953.
[17] *Ibid.*, October 5, 1954.

(*ch'ü*), and forty *hsiang*.[18] These autonomous areas already included a substantial proportion of Han Chinese; to further
enlarge the areas under the administration of autonomous
units would have resulted in the inclusion of a disproportion-
ately large number of Han Chinese. The establishment of the
provincial-level Kwangsi Chuang Autonomous Region in
1958 marked the extent to which the concept of regional autonomy could be stretched. While all of Kwangsi's non-Han
peoples were, of course, included in the autonomous region,
they were outnumbered two to one by the Han Chinese.

The three most populous national minorities in Kwangsi
after the Chuang are the Yao, Miao, and T'ung. Each of them
was favored with the establishment of an autonomous area.
The Ta-yao-shan Yao nationality autonomous *hsien*, established in May 1952, is the most important autonomous area
for the Yao people in Kwangsi. It served as a prototype for the

AUTONOMOUS HSIEN OF THE
KWANGSI CHUANG AUTONOMOUS REGION
*Tung-hsing was transferred to Kwangsi adminstrative control in 1965.

18 *Jen-min jih-pao*, April 6, 1954.

TABLE 2

National Minority	1954 Population (est.)	Autonomous Area	Date Established
		Lung-sheng Mult.	1951
Yao	440,000	Ta-yao-shan	1952
Miao	180,000	Ta-miao-shan	1953
T'ung	140,000	San-chiang T'ung	1952
		Lung-lin Mult.	1953

other autonomous *hsien* being established in the province. Embracing parts of three special districts, this area was reported to have a total population of 26,000, of which 18,000 were Yao. It was finally pacified in March 1951 after having been used as a base for bands of Nationalist troops, which were said to have caused serious disturbances. In August it was visited by the CPG's investigation team, which led the people there in establishing a Ta-yao-shan "unity pact" (*t'uan-chieh kung-yüeh*).[19] Preliminary efforts at political organization were entrusted to a Ta-yao-shan Work Committee. The Committee consisted of local cadres together with a task force despatched by the provincial government.[20] More than ninety cadres took part in the work in Liu-tuan village, which served as a pilot project. After spending two weeks in Liu-tuan, the cadres fanned out into the other thirty-eight villages comprising the autonomous area.[21] In conformity with the doctrine of regional autonomy, political power was first established in each of the thirty-nine villages, and then, at the next administrative level, in each of the area's six districts, before culminating in a people's government at the *hsien* level. In the course of this work, the political consciousness of the masses was heightened and 1,315 cadres were recruited. Of the sixteen leading functionaries of the various district governments, fifteen were Yao. After four months of preliminary work, the first session of the Ta-yao-shan All-Nationalities Representa-

[19] *Nan-fang jih-pao*, October 5, 1952.
[20] *Chang-chiang jih-pao*, June 16, 1952.
[21] *Nan-fang jih-pao*, June 2, 1952.

tive Congress convened on May 28 and elected a people's government for the autonomous *hsien*. The congress met at Chin-hsiu, the *hsien* capital.[22]

The other autonomous areas of Kwangsi which were established during 1952/53 were the Lung-lin Multinational autonomous *hsien*, the San-chiang T'ung nationality autonomous *hsien*, and the Ta-miao-shan Miao nationality autonomous *hsien*. Unlike Ta-yao-shan, these three autonomous *hsien* fell within the West Kwangsi Chuang autonomous area and came under its administrative jurisdiction. The Lung-sheng Multinational autonomous *hsien* (1951) and the two Yao nationality *hsien* of Tu-an (1955) and Pa-ma (1956) were established too early or too late to be of prime interest here, while the two autonomous *hsien* of southeast Kwangsi were initially formed as part of Kwangtung.

Lung-lin (literally, "vast forest"), bordering on Yunnan and Kweichow, is Kwangsi's largest *hsien*, measuring 500 *li* from east to west and 400 *li* from north to south.[23] Seven nationalities, the largest of which were the Miao, Yao, Chuang, and Han, made up its population of 190,000.[24] According to the secretary of the CCP committee for Lung-lin, the consciousness of the masses rose tremendously in the course of the creation of the autonomous *hsien*. The people's government for the *hsien* came into existence on the first day of 1953. Subordinate to the *hsien* administration, people's governments were established in each of Lung-lin's four districts and thirty-five *hsiang*.[25] As in the San-chiang area, the work of creating autonomous government in Lung-lin followed the suppression of banditry by the PLA and the arrival of CPG inspection teams.

Like the Lung-lin area, San-chiang is a region of "many mountains and few fields." Bordering on Kweichow and Hunan, San-chiang had a population of 202,000 in 1953, of which

[22] *Chang-chiang jih-pao*, June 16, 1952.
[23] *Kuang-hsi jih-pao*, January 21, 1953. A *li* is half a kilometer.
[24] *Ibid.*, June 11, 1954.
[25] Ch'en Hsi-ku, "Lung-lin ko-tsu lien-ho tzu-ch'ih ch'ü i nien lai ti ch'eng-chiu" (Lung-lin multinational coalition autonomous area's one year of accomplishments), *Ibid.*, October 3, 1953.

the T'ung comprised forty-six percent; other peoples represented were Chuang, Han, Yao, and Miao.[26] The Han Chinese in San-chiang must have numbered about 50,000 since the *national minority* population of the *hsien* was given elsewhere as 150,000.[27] The people's government of the San-chiang T'ung nationality autonomous area was elected by the 277 delegates to the *hsien*'s "all-nationalities, all-circles, people's representative congress," which met for its first session on December 3, 1952. The establishment of the autonomous area government for San-chiang *hsien* brought to a climax eight months of political work which appears to have been under the direction of the United Front Work Department's local office in the CCP bureau for I-shan special district, in which the *hsien* is located. The local United Front Work Department boss, Li Chih-ying, made the journey from his office in Liuchou, administrative seat of I-shan special district, to attend the opening session of the San-chiang people's congress.[28]

The Ta-miao-shan Miao nationality autonomous *hsien* was formally established at the second session of the area's "all-nationalities, all-circles, people's representative congress" which met at Jung-hsien, principal town of the area, from November 18 to 26, 1952. The 285 delegates at the meeting had been selected to represent every nationality, locality, and class. The Ta-miao-shan area, which was to become a new *hsien*, comprised 10 districts and 135 *hsiang* taken from 3 pre-existing *hsien*. The population of the area at that time was 160,000, of whom 70,000 were Miao. The balance was made up by six other nationalities: Han, Chuang, T'ung, Yao, Shui-chia, and Kao-shan. Representatives of the various nationalities used their own languages at the meeting, and exhibitions of their national dances were put on for the benefit of the mainly Han residents of Jung-hsien city. Li Chih-ying, of the United Front Work Department, was once again prominent among the participants. The decision to establish an autonomous area had apparently been made in July at a Kwangsi province nation-

---

[26] *Jen-min jih-pao*, January 14, 1953.
[27] *Kuang-hsi jih-pao*, May 30, 1952.
[28] *Ibid.*, December 21, 1952.

ality work conference, reportedly in response to "demands from the people of each nationality of Ta-miao-shan."[29]

The published reports concerning the establishment of autonomous areas in Kwangsi seldom reveal the tight control exercised by the state bureaucracy over the entire movement. Occasionally, however, the almost hidden force of the Party and Government reveals itself, giving logical cohesion to a process which has the appearance of developing spontaneously. For instance, at a Kwangsi province nationalities work conference which ended on June 25, 1952, it was resolved that in the second half of the year autonomous *hsien* should be created in the San-chiang, Ta-miao-shan, and Lung-lin areas.[30] This work conference was undoubtedly implementing decisions reached by the CPG in accordance with the findings of its inspection teams, for frequent mention is made of the fact that the work of implementing regional autonomy began in earnest in July, following the visits of the CPG teams. This strengthens the hypothesis suggested earlier that the implementation of regional autonomy in the Ta-yao-shan area, completed in May, was to serve as a pilot project for Kwangsi. Thus, it can be seen that by June of 1952 a program for the creation of the various *hsien*-level autonomous units in the province, established several months later, had already been endorsed. Part of the responsibility for implementing this program was passed on to officials at the special-district level—Pai-se, in the case of Lung-lin, and I-shan for San-chiang and Ta-miao-shan. This work must have been well underway by the time of the October Kwangsi nationalities work conference, which gave formal consideration to the General Program. Clearly, the General Program—promulgated, it will be recalled, in August—was based on a considerable accumulation of experience with regional autonomy in different parts of the country.

The way in which regional autonomy for national minorities was implemented in Kwangsi may be reviewed by looking briefly at the example of the Shih-wan-shan area in southeast-

[29] *Jen-min jih-pao*, December 19, 1952, and *Wen-hui-pao* (Hong Kong), December 13, 1952.

[30] *Kuang-hsi jih-pao*, July 24, 1952.

ern Kwangsi (subsequently ceded to Kwangtung). The June work conference had also decided that an autonomous area embracing the two *hsien* of Fang-cheng and Shang-szu should be established in the Shih-wan-shan moutain range.[31] This project was launched among the 13,000 P'ien, Yao, and Han inhabitants of the T'ung-chung district of Fang-cheng *hsien*. A work team was despatched by the Nationalities Affairs Commission of Kwangsi province to assist the local people in formulating their demands for regional autonomy. The provincial work team was reinforced by cadres sent by Ch'ing-chou special district. Local cadres from T'ung-chung also participated. From August 9 to 12, a preparatory conference was held at Na-liang, near the Vietnamese frontier. All the provincial, special-district, and local cadres who had been involved in the preliminary work attended the conference. They totaled seventy-seven persons. Also in attendance were village cadres and representatives of the local P'ien, Yao, and Han communities: taken together, they numbered sixty-nine persons.[32]

Following the meeting, the movement for regional autonomy was carried forward in the villages of T'ung-chung district, beginning in Pan-meng and Na-pa. The main preoccupations of the movements' executors were to propagate Chairman Mao's nationalities policy, stir up the masses, develop production, and promote nationalities unity. In the course of this work in T'ung-chung district, 80 villagers were selected as representatives for the future congress, while more than 400 were given training. In October, the T'ung-chung district joined with the other districts of Fang-cheng *hsien* to form the Shih-wan-shan P'ien and Yao nationalities autonomous area.[33]

The implementation of regional autonomy in Fang-cheng reveals the same pattern as that observed earlier in connection with the establishment of the Ta-yao-shan autonomous area: (1) detailed planning at each stage of the operation; (2) the influx of specially trained cadres from outside; (3) the selection

[31] *Ibid.*
[32] *Kuang-hsi jih-pao*, August 26, 1952.
[33] *Nan-fang jih-pao*, October 30, 1952.

ADMINISTRATIVE DIVISIONS OF YUNNAN IN 1955
(Autonomous areas are in bold-face type;
the others are special districts.)

of a pilot project location, with subsequent extension of the movement to the entire area; (4) induced participation of the local non-Han-Chinese people; (5) emphasis on training local cadres in the course of the operation; and (6) utilization of a composite and flexible "nationalities work team" (*min-tsu kung-tso tui*) as an arm of the provincial authorities.

THE HSI-SHUANG PAN-NA T'AI AUTONOMOUS AREA

Yunnan's T'ai people had a 1953 population of about half a million, of whom 300,000 lived in two autonomous areas established in that year.[34] The first, the Hsi-shuang Pan-na [Sip-song Pan-na] T'ai nationality autonomous area (SSPN), embraces the Mekong River and its tributaries in the southern extremity of Yunnan. It was formerly a semi-independent state whose people were referred to as T'ai Lü. The other, the Te-hung T'ai and Ching-p'o nationality autonomous area (THTCP), embraces the Salween and its tributaries in the extreme southwestern portion of the province. Foreign writers customarily referred to this area as the "Chinese Shan states" because of the similarities between it and the Shan states of Burma. Historically, the THTCP area, lying on the main trade route to Burma, had been more subject to Chinese influence than had the more isolated SSPN area. In 1953, Han Chinese made up twenty-five percent of the THTCP's population, whereas in the SSPN area the Chinese element was almost nil. Meng-tze, a largely Han Chinese town, became the administrative center of the THTCP when it was founded in July 1953.[35] The capital of the SSPN, established in January of the same year, was the tiny administrative outpost of Ch'e-li. In the summer of 1954 it was redesignated Yün-ch'ing-hung, its traditional T'ai name (as transliterated into Chinese), which means "city of dawn."[36] A large proportion of Yunnan's T'ai people who are not found in the SSPN or THTCP inhabit the country lying between these two autonomous areas. The T'ai in this region are sometimes referred to as T'ai Nüa. They live in isolated river valleys interspersed among hills dominated by the K'awa and Lahu uplanders.

The SSPN was formally established by the first session of the area's "all-nationalities, all-circles, people's representative congress," which met in Ch'e-li from January 17 to 23. No fewer than 47 different ethno-linguistic groups had been identified within the SSPN area, and it was claimed that all of them were represented among the 416 delegates to the congress. Leading members of the standing committee and government council

[34] *Jen-min jih-pao*, September 15, 1954.

[35] *Ibid.*, August 1, 1953.

[36] A Yün-pien, *Hsi-shuang pan-na ho t'ai-tsu* (The Sip-song Pan-na and the T'ai people) (Peking, 1961), p. 37.

elected by the congress represented T'ai, Aini, P'u-man, and Han nationalities as well as the Buddhist clergy. An outstanding feature of the autonomous area government was the prominence in it of members of the pre-Communist ruling elite, denoted in Chinese sources by the surname Chao, or (in T'ai) "chief." Thus, Chao Ts'un-hsin became Chairman of the government, and three of the five vice-chairmen were also called Chao.[37]

Despite this appearance of indigenous leadership, the preparatory work which preceded the formal establishment of the SSPN suggests a political structure not so different from that of the autonomous areas which were established contemporaneously in Kwangsi. Early in 1951, the provincial government in Kunming had set up an organizational framework for the autonomous area and despatched a "nationalities work team" of over two hundred persons. The work team included students from the SSPN area who had completed training at the Nationalities Institute in Kunming. One T'ai nationality autonomous *hsiang* was created in each of three *hsien* to serve as models for the entire area. At the same time, an extensive propaganda campaign was carried out to introduce the people to the concepts of the CCP's national minority policy. On January 1, 1953, the preparatory committee held a general meeting at which all questions relating to the establishment of the autonomous area were taken up: the composition of its government was discussed and its name and boundaries decided. The SSPN embraced four *hsien* in their entirety and parts of four others. Altogether, it included 24 districts with a total area of 25,000 square kilometers. However, the CCP chose to emphasize the *pan-na*, the units traditionally comprising the Sip-song Pan-na (twelve *pan-na*), as the administrative unit of the autonomous area.[38]

The first session of the SSPN people's congress which convened later in the month to endorse the work of the preparatory committee exchanged congratulatory greetings with regional and national authorities. In its telegram to Chairman

[37] *Ta-kung-pao* (Tientsin), February 1, 1953.
[38] *Ibid.*

Mao, the congress said that under the brilliant light of the CCP's nationalities policy, all the peoples of the SSPN had become united, making possible the creation of the autonomous area. The establishment of the SSPN, the congress said, opened up an unprecedentedly bright future for its people and their descendants. It noted that the congress had endorsed a "pact of patriotism and nationalities unity" (*min-tsu t'uan-chieh ai-kuo kung-yüeh*). In its program for the next two years, the autonomous area promised to increase production and to support the PLA. In its message to the Army, the SSPN emphasized the significance for national defense of its position on the extreme southern frontier of the motherland and pledged itself to imbibe the spirit of the PLA's successes in Korea and to remain vigilant.[39]

The impression that united-front tactics were of special importance in the establishment of the SSPN is reinforced by the fact that the creation of a new administrative system at the local level followed rather than preceded the formal launching of the autonomous area. People's governments at the district level were set up in four of the area's *pan-na* during June and July 1953—that is, half a year after the founding of the SSPN itself. At the same time, a district-level autonomous government was established for the Aini, one of the SSPN's sub-minorities. Creation of these local administrative units followed intensive work among the people, culminating in the convening of *pan-na* "all-nationalities, all-circles, people's representative congresses." The main ingredient of the propaganda was the ideology of self-government for nationalities as espoused by the CCP. The propaganda and other work connected with the creation of these local governments was directed by cadres sent down from higher levels, not only from the SSPN government but also from the authorities of Sze-mao special district. The *pan-na* people's congresses telegraphed greetings to Chairman Mao and concluded "patriotic unity pacts," just as the SSPN people's congress had done.[40]

Like the four *pan-na* governments, the Ke-lang-ho Aini na-

[39] *Ibid.*
[40] *Yün-nan jih-pao,* September 4, 1953.

tionality autonomous area people's government was established under the guidance of people's governments at superior levels, as well as of the nationalities work team of Yunnan province. Its establishment conformed to a plan drawn up by the SSPN people's government for the carrying out of regional autonomy for the sub-minorities within the autonomous area. Ke-lang-ho is a mountainous district on the border between the two *hsien* of Ch'e-li and Fu-hai. Its population of 8,900 included small numbers of Han and Lahu in addition to the Aini, who predominated. The newly elected Aini chairman of the Ke-lang-ho people's government declared that: "Henceforth the Aini people will enthusiastically welcome and deeply appreciate help extended by the elder-brother Han and T'ai nationalities; under the leadership of higher administrative echelons, together improve production and safeguard national defense."[41]

THE TE-HUNG T'AI AND CHING-P'O AUTONOMOUS AREA

The Te-hung T'ai and Ching-p'o nationalities autonomous area (THTCP) was formally established by the first session of the area's "all-nationalities, all-circles, people's representative congress," which met from July 18 to 24, 1953 at Mang-shih. The autonomous area's 400,000 people were represented by 385 delegates. The Yunnan CCP bureau was represented at the congress by the vice-chairman of the provincial people's government, Kuo Ying-ch'in; also in attendance were the assistant secretary of the Yunnan CCP bureau's frontier committee and the secretary of the CCP committee for the Pao-shan area. The THTCP people's government elected by the congress was headed by Tao Ching-pan as chairman. Of seven vice-chairmen, three were T'ai, like Tao himself; three were Ching-p'o; and one was Han. A similar national distribution characterized the top membership of the standing committee of the THTCP people's congress. The congress concluded a "pact of patriotism and nationalities unity" (*ko-tsu jen-min ai-kuo t'uan-chieh kung-yüeh*) and listened to orations by Kuo Ying-ch'in as well as by

[41] *Ibid.*

Chairman Tao and other "leading personalities of each nationality having close connections with the masses."[42]

As the *Yunnan Daily* noted editorially, the main function of the first session of the THTCP people's congress was to ratify work which had already been thoroughly done in preparation for the establishment of the autonomous area.[43] During this preparatory stage, relations between the THTCP's 97,000 Ching-p'o hill farmers and 175,000 T'ai lowlanders were said to have improved, while over 800 revolutionary cadres of various nationalities were trained. According to the editorial, this instance of the successful implementation of the policy of regional autonomy demonstrated the efficacy of a broad united-front tactic in frontier regions which had ties with contiguous non-Chinese areas. All "anti-imperialist and patriotic" elements, including *t'u-ssu*; officials for hill areas (*shan-kuan*) inherited from the *ancien regime*; headmen; and Buddhist clergy had been brought into the new polity.[44]

The preparatory work for the THTCP was concentrated in Lü-hsi *hsien*, which served the CCP as a pilot-project area. The administrative center for Lü-hsi is the town of Mang-shih, which was to become the capital of the THTCP. Contingents of the provincial nationalities work team (*min-tsu kung-tso tui*) assigned to Lü-hsi used the regional center of Pao-shan as a staging area, just as Meng-tzu was the base for preparatory work in the SSPN. The political work of the nationalities work team in Lü-hsi, which began in August 1952, was accompanied by the extension of aid to the local non-Han peoples. Among the T'ai lowlanders, medical work was stressed, while distributions of grain took precedence in work with the Shan-t'ou (Karen) hill people, an important sub-minority group of Lü-hsi. In its task of imposing a new political order on Lü-hsi, the nationalities work team gave first priority to patriotic education, and the hill peoples of the frontier were singled out for special attention. The team apparently succeeded in convincing the headmen of the Shan-t'ou and Peng-lung uplanders

[42] *Yün-nan jih-pao*, August 8, 1953.
[43] *Ibid.*
[44] *Ibid.*

that the CCP was preferable to the "Kuomintang reactionary gang" or the "Japanese devils." In its efforts to instill patriotism among the T'ai lowlanders, the team provided political indoctrination for the Buddhist clergy.[45]

As in the SSPN, however, the political reorganization of the THTCP could not be completed prior to the time of its formal establishment in July 1953. At the end of June 1954—that is, two years after the commencement of preparatory work in the THTCP and a year after its establishment—the new political order had still not been established in half the townships of the autonomous area. They still required systematic work. Under CCP and government leadership, a program was initiated in July 1954 to strengthen political work in these "weak" areas by transferring experience and personnel from "strong" areas. It was envisioned that 2,900 "positive elements" would receive training in the second half of the year. They were to be recruited from villages in the "weak" areas, and would be returned to them after training. It was hoped that this crash program would correct the shortage of cadres that was a basic cause of the "uneven" development of the THTCP area.

BETWEEN THE SALWEEN AND THE MEKONG

In the hilly country lying between the THTCP and the SSPN, the Chinese Communists found a number of peoples living in isolated communities. Much of the area was dominated by K'awa (Wa) and Lahu uplanders, but T'ai communities were found in the small river valleys which descend into Burma. The several hsien-level autonomous areas established in this area by the CCP roughly corresponded to its ethnic configuration.

The Lan-tsang [Mekong] Lahu autonomous area was established in April 1953 on the occasion of the first session of its "all-nationalities, all-circles, people's representative congress." The 272 delegates at the congress represented 17 different nationalities with a total population of 200,000. The most important national groups were the Lahu (46 percent of the total), Han, Aini, K'awa, Yi, T'ai, and P'u-man. The second secre-

[45] *Ibid.*, November 15, 1952.

tary of the local CCP committee spoke to the congress about the preparatory work which had made possible the creation of the autonomous area, and the newly elected Lahu chairman of the autonomous area government discussed the tasks of the coming two years. In attendance were official guests from different parts of Yunnan and from other provinces; the SSPN, which borders on the Lan-tsang area, sent a 28-man delegation. Situated on the west bank of the Lan-tsang River, this Lahu autonomous area comprised two districts of the former Lan-tsang *hsien* plus two districts from Ning-chiang *hsien*, together with an area known as K'awa-shan (K'awa Mountain) district. Its total area was 10,100 square kilometers. We know from non-Communist sources that the region of the Lan-tsang Lahu autonomous area, and the K'awa-shan in particular, was dominated by Nationalist forces under Li Mi for an extended period in 1951/52. Only in the winter of 1952/53 was the K'awa-shan area penetrated by public security forces (*kung-an-pu*).[46] It is not surprising, therefore, that the question of frontier security, and the role of the PLA in making possible the establishment of the autonomous area, were emphasized at the congress.[47]

The Meng-lien T'ai, Lahu, and K'awa nationalities autonomous area was established in June 1954. It is located on the Burma border, with the SSPN to the east and the Lan-tsang Lahu area to the north. The government elected by the first session of the "all-nationalities, all-circles, people's representative congress" of the Meng-lien area was headed by a T'ai chairman and Lahu, K'awa, Han, and T'ai vice-chairmen. An active role at the congress was played by the secretary of the Sze-mao region CCP committee, who delivered a speech on the subject of the PRC's draft constitution. Other organizations represented included the CCP's Lan-tsang border work committee (*Chung-kung lan-tsang pien-chiang kung-tso wei-yüan-hui*) and the Nationalities Affairs Commission for the southwest region (*Hsi-nan min-tsu shih-wu wei-yüan-hui*). Also on hand

[46] *Ibid.*, November 21, 1953.
[47] *Jen-min jih-pao*, April 18, 1953.

were delegations from the West Kwangsi Chuang nationality autonomous area, the SSPN, and other autonomous areas. The population of the Meng-lien region itself, numbering 35,000 people, were represented by 125 delegates at the congress. The autonomous area embraced four districts, with a total area of 1,775 square kilometers.[48]

A third autonomous area established in the wild territory stretching between the THTCP and SSPN areas was the Keng-ma T'ai and K'awa nationalities autonomous area. Although it was not formally constituted as a legal entity until 1956, a preparatory committee for the area was set up in March 1954. Like the K'awa-shan region of the Lan-tsang Lahu autonomous area, Keng-ma had been subject to heavy pressure from Li Mi's Nationalist troops. The preparatory committee had a T'ai chairman and a K'awa vice-chairman. Between July and September 1954, it was claimed, 182 local cadres were trained. All questions relating to the establishment of the autonomous area were discussed by cadres of Meng-lien *hsien* at a meeting sponsored by the local CCP committee.[49]

THE HUNG-HO HANI NATIONALITY AUTONOMOUS AREA

The Hung-ho [Red River] Hani nationality autonomous area (HHHN) covers 10,000 square kilometers of territory situated in the angle of the Red River, to the north and east, and the Vietnamese frontier, to the south. Three existing *hsien* plus a small amount of additional territory were merged to form the HHHN, which was rated administratively as an autonomous area of the special-district (later, *chou*) level. Its population of 400,000 included ten or more national groups. The Hani, with 240,000 people, were the most numerous. The name "Hani" was officially adopted at the time of the establishment of the HHHN to denote the people earlier referred to by the name Aini. In Western literature the peoples found in Indochina and Burma who are related to the Hani of Yunnan are usually called Akha. Other major groups were the Ti,

[48] *Yün-nan jih-pao,* July 5, 1954.
[49] *Ibid.,* December 23, 1954.

T'ai, Miao, Yao, and Han. The territory of the HHHN is hilly, with only a very limited area being suitable for wet-rice agriculture.[50]

The HHHN was officially established on January 1, 1954, at the conclusion of the first session of the area's "all-nationalities, all-circles, people's representative congress," held at Yüan-yang, capital of the HHHN. The more than 400 delegates who attended the congress represented not only the various nationalities of the HHHN but also the Army, Government, and Party. The Frontier Defense Corps (*pien-fang pu-tui*) was the section of the PLA most directly concerned. The assistant secretary of the Yunnan province CCP's Frontier Work Committee (*pien-chiang kung-tso wei-yüan-hui*) attended the congress, as did the vice-chairman of the provincial government's Nationalities Affairs Commission. Also represented was the CCP committee of Meng-tzu special district, adjacent to the HHHN. The congress received reports from the autonomous area's preparatory committee and the provincial Nationality Affairs Commission; the CCP's Hung-ho Region Frontier Work Committee (*hung-ho ch'ü pien kung hui*) presented a report on four years of nationality work in the Hung-ho area. These various reports were discussed by the delegates in small groups (*hsiao-tsu*) as well as in plenary session. The congress elected an HHHN people's government council of 32 persons headed by a Hani Chairman; a 34-man standing committee of the people's congress was also chosen, a Yi being elected as its chairman. The congress gave its endorsement to a code governing the organization and functioning of the HHHN people's government and approved a "pact of unity and patriotism" (*t'uan-chieh ai-kuo kung-yüeh*). Looking toward the future, the delegates undertook, among other things, to strengthen unity among the HHHN's nationalities and to increase production. The congress addressed a telegram to "Beloved Chairman Mao" expressing appreciation for the guidance provided by his nationalities policy.[51]

---

[50] *Kuang-ming jih-pao*, January 6, 1954; *Jen-min jih-pao*, January 6, 1954.

[51] *Yün-nan jih-pao*, January 13, 1954.

Creation of the HHHN was the fruit of several years of effort, both military and political. Nationalist guerrillas had lodged themselves on the frontier and were difficult to root out. In July 1953 a nationalities work team arrived in Hung-ho *hsien* from Meng-tzu and began operating in a number of separate villages. The decision to go ahead with the establishment of the HHHN was reached at a nationalities work conference called in September by the Nationalities Affairs Commission of Meng-tzu special district.[52]

Cadre recruitment and the development of trade were important parts of the preparatory phase in the creation of the HHHN: by the time of its formal establishment, nearly 3,000 national minority cadres had been processed. Those selected included "patriotic intellectuals," "positive elements" from the masses, and traditional leaders having "connections with the masses." Some of them were sent to national minority institutes at national, regional (southwest), or provincial level. Among the special courses offered were tree crops, irrigation, and health. These 3,000 national minority cadres made up 27 percent of the total number of cadres in the HHHN at the time of its founding, the rest being Han Chinese. A trade development company (*mao-i chih kung-ssu*) was established in 1951. The company was supplemented by 15 trading teams (*hsiao-tsu*) which penetrated into remote areas, buying local products in exchange for manufactured articles. Stores were established at key points.[53]

THE NU-CHIANG LISU NATIONALITY AUTONOMOUS AREA

The Nu-chiang [Salween River] Lisu nationality autonomous area (NCLS) is situated on the upper Salween River, just north of the Te-hung T'ai and Ching-p'o area. It was formally established on August 23, 1954, at the conclusion of the first session of the area's "all-nationalities, all-circles, people's representative congress," which met at the autonomous area's capital of Pi-chiang. The 367 delegates at the congress represented twelve nationalities, notably Lisu, Nu, Tu-lung, Yi,

[52] *Ibid.*, September 23, 1953.
[53] *Ibid.*, January 13, 1954.

Min-chia, and Han. A Lisu was elected chairman of the NCLS government, while other nationalities were represented among the vice-chairmen. The deputy head of the Nationalities Affairs Commission (*Min-tsu shih-wu wei-yüan-hui*) for Yunnan province addressed the congress, which also heard reports on past work experience and future tasks and passed a resolution in support of the draft constitution of the PRC. The provincial government and party organizations, as well as other autonomous areas, sent observers or telegraphic greetings to the congress.[54]

Commenting editorially on the establishment of the NCLS, the *Yunnan Daily* noted that creation of the new autonomous area followed the establishment of the Hsi-shuang Pan-na T'ai, Te-hung T'ai and Ching-p'o, and Hung-ho Hani nationality autonomous areas, all of which were situated on Yunnan's frontier.[55] This event, the editorial said, would greatly strengthen nationalities unity and create closer relations between the central authorities and the frontier regions. In the space of four years, 439 local cadres had been recruited and trained, but the role of Han and other "outside" cadres in the development of the NCLS was still important.

RECAPITULATION AND CONCLUSION

The establishment of the four major autonomous areas in Yunnan discussed above resulted in the administrative delimitation of most of the province's frontier. Table 3 summarizes the basic data on these four areas, the SSPN (Sip-song Pan-na), THTCP (Te-hung T'ai and Ching-p'o), HHHN (Hung-ho Hani), and NCLS (Nu-chiang Lisu). In the work of establishing, and in the subsequent control of, each of these areas, the CCP based itself on centers of Han Chinese population, where its position was felt to be relatively secure. In the SSPN and THTCP,

54 *Jen-min jih-pao*, September 2, 1954.
55 "T'uan-chieh, sheng-ch'an, chin-pu, wei chu-pu kuo-tu tao she-wei chu-i erh fen-tou—ch'ing-chu nu-chiang li-su tsu tzu-ch'ih ch'ü chien-li" (Struggle determinedly for unity, production, and progress, in order to advance in the transition to socialism—congratulating the establishment of the Nu-chiang Li-su Nationality autonomous area), *Yün-nan jih-pao*, September 9, 1954.

TABLE 3

Autonomous Area	Date Established	Administrative Level	Capital
SSPN	January 1953	special district	Yün-ching-hung
THTCP	July 1953	special district	Meng-shih
HHHN	January 1954	special district	Yüan-yang
NCLS	August 1954	special district	Pi-chiang

which occupy pivotal positions on the frontier, the CCP used Pu-erh and Pao-shan, respectively, as staging areas. These two cities, in turn, were operationally dependent upon the provincial capital, Kunming. Yün-ch'ing-hung and Meng-shih, the administrative centers of the SSPN and THTCP, were the CCP's forward positions, dependent on Pu-erh and Pao-shan, respectively. In the case of the HHHN, Meng-tzu provided the staging area. The pattern with respect to the NCLS is less clear, though it appears that both Li-chiang and Pao-shan were of some importance.

Only in 1958 did the fifth and last of Yunnan's frontier autonomous areas of the special-district level come into existence, the Wen-shan Chuang and Miao autonomous *chou* (WSCM). The birth of the WSCM was contemporaneous with the metamorphosis of the West Kwangsi Chuang autonomous *chou* into the province-level Kwangsi Chuang autonomous region (*ch'ü*). These developments will be considered in the next chapter. The WSCM had close economic and ethnic ties with Kwangsi, with which it has a common border. In the south, it borders on Vietnam. Also in 1958, the Ts'ang-yuan K'awa autonomous *hsien* was established in the frontier zone lying between the THTCP and the SSPN, completing the administrative structure of this part of the frontier. By 1954, nevertheless, Yunnan's most sensitive frontier areas—those with Burma and Laos—had, in the main, been formed into autonomous areas (SSPN, THTCP, HHHN, and NCLS) at the special-district level; in addition, there were the three *hsien*-level autonomous areas in the predominantly T'ai and K'awa country between the THTCP and the SSPN. Another *hsien*-level unit, the Chiang-ch'eng Hani and Yi autonomous area, situated between the SSPN and the HHHN, was established in May 1954. Finally, the Kung-shan Tu-lung and Nu autonomous *hsien* (1956) was established in the extreme northwestern corner of Yunnan, between the NCLS and the Tibetan border. (See map, page 90.)

In Han Chinese areas, the political power of the CCP rested largely on its demonstrated willingness to take wealth from the rich and give it to the poor. This was much less true in non-Han-Chinese areas, where the CCP's primary concern was with the promotion of solidarity between the Han and the national minorities. The wealth distributed to the masses in national minority areas frequently came from the reserves of the state rather than from any surplus within their own societies. Thus, it involved a transfer of wealth from Han to non-Han areas and was therefore a token of CCP good faith vis-à-vis the minorities. This policy of state assistance to national minority areas was especially important in frontier regions having ties with the external world. Gifts of grain, seed, and tools were a regular feature of the preparatory work that preceded the establishment of autonomous areas both in Yunnan and Kwangsi. State-controlled commerce, manipulated so as to benefit national minority areas, was used for the same purpose.

Regional autonomy in the two provinces was implemented in accordance with plans drawn up by the central authorities. Representatives of the state had this plan with them when they began carrying out national minority work. Their task was to involve the native peoples in a process which was very largely pre-determined. Descriptions of the creation of autonomous areas are monotonously repetitive: convening of a representative people's congress which hears certain reports and passes certain items of legislation, election of a government council which reflects fairly precisely the ethnic composition of the area, despatch of a laudatory telegram to Chairman Mao. The agenda for the formalities pertaining to creation of an autonomous area is determined by the preparatory work team, which is composed principally of outsiders. In addition to party and government representatives, the work team includes a sizeable proportion of students from the provincial Nationalities Institute. Among these students would be found progressive individuals from the area in question who had previously been selected for training. The more politically sensitive the area, the greater the reliance on united-front tactics, in which the CCP tends to make use of traditional leaders and to de-emphasize mass movements. The chief responsibility of the autonomous area government following its establishment is, with Han Chinese help, to develop the economy of the area so as to give substance to the people's newly acquired political rights and to contribute to the progress of the national economy.

4

THE ESTABLISHMENT
OF AUTONOMOUS
AREAS: PHASE TWO

THE unfolding of the PRC's policy of regional autonomy for national minorities took the better part of a decade in Yunnan and Kwangsi. The initial phase of that process, occupying the first half of the 1950's, was described in the preceding chapter. The final stages of the same process, spanning the middle and late 1950's, remain to be dealt with. The principal event in Kwangsi during this latter period was the metamorphosis of the entire province into the Kwangsi Chuang Autonomous Region, one of five such regions to be established in the whole country. (The others, with their dates of establishment, are the Inner Mongolia Autonomous Region [1947], the Sinkiang Uighur Autonomous Region [1955], the Ninghsia Hui Autonomous Region [1958], and the Tibet Autonomous Region [1965].) With the creation of the Kwangsi Chuang Autonomous Region, the West Kwangsi Chuang autonomous *chou* ceased to function as a separate entity, but the various autonomous *hsien* already established in Kwangsi were not affected. In Yunnan, meanwhile, the second phase in the implementation of the PRC's policy of national regional autonomy was the establishment of autonomous *chou* and *hsien* in the interior, as distinguished from the frontier. These separate processes in Kwangsi and Yunnan, so different from one another, brought to completion the administrative restructuring implicit in the CCP's national minority policy. Once established, these various autonomous areas tended to lose their individuality as the whole country moved more rapidly in the direction of creating a highly integrated socialist state.

Establishment of the Kwangsi Chuang Autonomous Region

In October 1956, less than a year after the establishment of the Kwei-hsi Chuang autonomous *chou*, the plan to establish a province-level autonomous region for the Chuang was made public. In that month, the Kwangsi committee of the CCP, acting on a recommendation of the Central Committee, began pressing the idea both inside and outside the Party. In December, the Kwangsi People's Political Consultative Conference met to discuss this undertaking.[1] The three-day meeting was attended by 150 regular members of the Kwangsi branch of the Chinese People's Political Consultative Conference (CPPCC) plus 120 specially invited representatives. Hsiao I-chou, Vice-chairman of the Kwangsi People's Government, presented his "Report on How to Resolve the Question of a Kwangsi Chuang Autonomous Region." He indicated that during the preceding half year the People's Democratic United Front had developed a great deal of strength in the province.[2] Hsiao noted that there had been important accomplishments in implementing the Party's and Government's national minority policy in Kwangsi, but that there had been many (unspecified) shortcomings. The establishment of an autonomous area at the provincial level would, in his opinion, help to overcome these difficulties. A further argument in

[1] *Kuang-hsi jih-pao*, December 25, 1956.
[2] The United Front is the mode of operation of the CPPCC. The latter organization in turn is the public or overt body through which the CCP's United Front Work Department seeks to mobilize bourgeois elements for socialist ends. Traditional leaders among the national minorities fall into the category of bourgeois elements.

favor of a provincial-level autonomous area was the preservation of Kwangsi as an economic unit. The mountainous western part of the province contains important industrial raw materials, while Kwangsi's agricultural base is located in the eastern lowlands. Hsiao then posed a question the answer to which he had just provided: should all of Kwangsi be brought together as a single autonomous area, or should the province be divided in two? The latter method would create two province-level units: a Chuang autonomous area in the west and a truncated Kwangsi province in the east. These two ways of "solving" the problem came to be labeled as the "unite" (ho) form and the "divide" (fen) form. Needless to say, the CCP threw its weight behind the first, turning the effort into a mass campaign designed to expose, isolate, and destroy bourgeois, rightist, and counter-revolutionary sentiment in Kwangsi. In the same speech, Hsiao ridiculed apprehensions concerning the proposed Kwangsi Chuang Autonomous Region, which came to represent two poles of "erroneous" thinking against which CCP propaganda was directed. The first fear was that in the new polity the Han Chinese would have to learn the Chuang language: this turned into "great-Han chauvinism" (ta han-tsu chu-i). The second fear was that if Kwangsi were united, the Chuang area would be swamped by Han cadres: this tendency was made to look like "local nationalism" (ti-fang min-tsu chu-i).

Later in the meeting the participants split up into small groups for further discussion. These groups were organized according to the place of origin of the participants, the hsien being the standard unit per group. As a result of these small-group discussions, it was claimed, everyone was won over to the "unite" (ho) solution as opposed to the "divide" (fen) solution. At the conclusion of the meeting a general summary was given by the chairman of the Kwangsi branch of the CPPCC. He called upon the delegates to carry out propaganda work in favor of the proposed Kwangsi Chuang Autonomous Region when they returned home. A note of urgency was added to this plea when he observed that 1956 had been a bad year for agriculture in Kwangsi. Poor working style among CCP cadres (dogmatism, bureaucratism, sectarianism), as well as natural calamities, were held to blame.[3]

During 1957, meetings were held throughout the province to popularize (or, in the Chinese phrase, to "ferment"—*yün-niao t'ao-lun*) the idea of turning Kwangsi into an autonomous region. In this propaganda work, CCP cadres stressed the idea that as the national minority with the largest population in China it was *appropriate* for the Chuang to have a province-level autonomous area, as the Mongols and Uighurs did. It was noted that this was in keeping with the principles of the 1954 Constitution, and that it would be advantageous from the point of view of China's international relations. At "fermentation" meetings held in the east Kwangsi cities of Kweilin, Liuchow, and Wuchow, some people suggested that there was no real difference between Chuang and Han people, and that since the latter were much more numerous than the former, perhaps a Kwangsi Chuang Autonomous Region was not necessary. Naturally this view was rejected in the course of debate.[4] These were not mass meetings but restricted discussions attended by key individuals—the kind of people whom it was the task of the United Front Work Department of the CCP to organize. They were often referred to as meetings of "all nationalities and all circles," and included returned overseas Chinese among their participants. They were usually held in county (*hsien*) seats. Typically, reports of these meetings claimed that, after discussion, nearly everyone endorsed the "unite" approach as opposed to the "divide" approach to the establishment of a Kwangsi Chuang Autonomous Region.

Another argument put forward in these meetings to strengthen the case for the proposed autonomous area was that the Chuang people needed Han help in developing the rich natural resources found in their part of the province.[5] Yet another argument was that, although the Chuang were concen-

[3] *Kuang-hsi jih-pao*, December 25, 1956.

[4] *Ibid.*, January 19, 1957. There was also sentiment in favor of a union between Kwangtung and eastern Kwangsi, in the event that a Chuang autonomous area were retained in western Kwangsi.

[5] *Ibid.*, January 23, 1957.

trated in the Kwei-hsi Chuang autonomous *chou* in the western part of the province, where they constituted seventy percent of the population, Chuang were found in all parts of the province. It was claimed that if Kwangsi were an autonomous region it would be easier to protect their rights as a minority people.[6] In order to better lead discussions concerning the proposed autonomous region, CCP cadres in Kweilin were sent into the hills to spend some time with national minority peoples.[7]

It was found in the course of the "fermentation" work that the CCP's national minority policy was little understood among the people whom it wanted to persuade of the wisdom of establishing a Kwangsi Chuang Autonomous Region. Thus, many people believed that in the San-chiang multinational autonomous *hsien* there were two governments, one for the Han Chinese, and one for the national minorities. This resulted from confusing "national autonomy" with "regional autonomy." The Chairman of the Kwangsi province Nationalities Affairs Commission therefore called upon cadres to "intensify the teaching of the policy of national regional autonomy of the People's Republic of China, so that the necessity of establishing the Kwangsi Chuang Autonomous Region may be clearly understood."[8]

This whole propaganda effort was directed mainly at the Han residents of Kwangsi, or so the published data suggest. Apparently the national minorities, and the Chuang in particular, were willing if not anxious to see the province become an autonomous region. However, they seem not to have taken any active part in laying the groundwork for this change but, rather, to have remained passive spectators. It was in the Han Chinese areas of eastern Kwangsi, and in the Kweilin area more than elsewhere, that propaganda activity was most intense. There can be no doubt that the initiative for this effort came from outside the province and that the work was carried out by a CCP organization in Kwangsi which must have in-

[6] *Ibid.*, February 6, 1957.
[7] *Ibid.*, February 12, 1957.
[8] *Ibid.*, February 13, 1957.

cluded a large number of outsiders. The project does not seem to have been related to any real need, nor to any acute sense of dissatisfaction, felt within the province itself. The whole effort could have served only one vital political purpose: namely, the smashing of Kwangsi Han Chinese opposition to the Communist Party itself. This is not to say that the project may not have served other purposes as well—e.g., economic integration of the province, external propaganda, the full implementation of regional autonomy as laid down by the Constitution, and so on—but I believe that these purposes were secondary. The establishment of the Kwangsi Chuang Autonomous Region may be seen, then, as the *coup de grace* for the local Chinese in their struggle against the CCP. The CCP had found an ally in the Chuang, who, according to the testimony of a former resident of the province, were the main force in the provincial Party apparatus.[9]

In March 1957, a group of some fifty prominent persons (most of them Han Chinese) from Kwangsi were invited to Peking to participate in further discussions concerning the establishment of the Kwangsi Chuang Autonomous Region. In Peking they were joined by Kwangsi people living in other parts of China.[10] The discussions were held under the auspices of the CPPCC and lasted for ten days. Many of the delegates spoke at the meeting, and they heard a report by Premier Chou En-lai. Present at the meeting were leading lights of the CCP's United Front Work Department, including Li Wei-han, Vice-chairman of the CPPCC, and his deputy, Chang Chih-i, a Vice-chairman of the Nationalities Commission of the National People's Congress. Chang, a native of Kwangsi, was probably a key individual in the project to establish a Chuang autonomous region. In his speech, Premier Chou called for a more extensive propaganda effort in Kwangsi to reach the masses. With regard to this renewed propaganda effort, Chou said that the decision to transform Kwangsi province into a Chuang autonomous area (employing the "unite" method) had already

[9] Interview held in Hong Kong on May 17, 1967, with a Kwangsi man of mixed Han-Chuang parentage.
[10] *Jen-min jih-pao*, April 20, 1957.

been made and was no longer a matter for debate. However, no final decision had been made as to the name of the new administrative unit. It would probably be called the Kwangsi Chuang Autonomous Region, but the question could still be discussed.[11]

On May 4, 1957, the *People's Daily* carried a long article by Li Wei-han on "different perspectives and opinions concerning the question of a Chuang autonomous region."[12] This is probably the most complete public statement on the issue. Li wrote the article in his capacity as Chairman of the United Front Work Department of the Chinese Communist Party. He reiterated the various arguments in favor of the venture which have already been discussed. Several other points made by Li are worth mentioning here. He pointed out that Kwangsi's population was not very large in comparison with other Chinese provinces, so it should not be divided. He mentioned that Kwangsi had a history of six hundred years as a province, and that this history had been made not by Han Chinese alone but by Chuang people as well.[13] The present task of building socialism, he said, should give great impetus to Chuang-Han solidarity. He noted that many people objected to the term "Kwangsi Chuang Autonomous Region" because it did not mention the Han, who comprised, after all, a majority of Kwangsi's population. One of the more interesting alternative suggestions which had been made was "South Yüeh Autonomous Region," *yüeh* being an old term for Kwangtung and Kwangsi. However, Li argued forcefully for the adoption of the officially sponsored name.

The first session of the First Kwangsi CCP Congress was held in June 1956. At its second session, held from April 26 to May 9, 1957, the project to establish a Kwangsi Chuang Autonomous Region was joined with the anti-rightist campaign then sweeping the country.[14] From that time on opponents of the project were branded as counter-revolutionaries. At the end of

[11] *Ibid.*, April 20, 1957.
[12] *Ibid.*, May 4, 1957; *Kuang-hsi jih-pao*, May 5, 1957.
[13] The Chuang have resided in the Kwangsi area since the stone age.
[14] *Kuang-hsi jih-pao*, May 11, 1957.

the meeting, the Kwangsi CCP Committee issued a resolution endorsing the initiative taken earlier by the Central Committee in proposing the establishment of a province-level Chuang autonomous region and calling on everyone in Kwangsi to actively support this project.[15] By the following month it was claimed that "fermentation" meetings had been held throughout the province. It was said that 17,747 delegates had discussed the problem in people's congresses convened in the province's five cities and seventy *hsien*.[16] In June it was revealed that for some time the Kwei-hsi Chuang autonomous *chou* had been cut off from effective contact with the Central Committee by obstructionist tactics on the part of the province-level administrators, who were also accused of interfering in the internal administration of the *chou*. One particular bone of contention between the province and the *chou* was control of tax funds.[17]

The principal rightist singled out for attack by the CCP was Huang Shao-pan. The CCP accused Huang of holding the following views concerning the projected Kwangsi autonomous region which were contrary to its own: first, the name of the new unit should contain the word "province," because, unlike the term "autonomous area," it had content; second, Kwangsi did not really have any national minorities because the groups so identified had long since been absorbed by the Han Chinese; third, before setting up an autonomous region, the effects upon the Han people should be examined, for if they were prevented from traveling freely or from putting up signs in Chinese characters they would oppose the government, thus creating a situation that could be exploited by Taiwan; fourth, proposing the use, without admitting prior CCP propaganda, of bourgeois-style elections to test the sentiments of the Han masses toward the projected autonomous region; fifth, Han Chinese feelings needed to be given more attention and sympathy. Huang was further abused because, as a member of the Kwangsi delegation that went to Peking at the invitation of

[15] *Ibid.*
[16] *Ibid.*, June 14, 1957.
[17] *Ibid.*, June 7, 1957.

the CPPCC, he had been unwilling to return to Kwangsi. On this same trip, the Kwangsi delegation had visited the Inner Mongolia Autonomous Region, but, taking exception to the lesson the CCP wanted the delegates to learn from this visit, Huang insisted that the historical conditions of Inner Mongolia were completely different from those of Kwangsi.[18]

Whereas Huang Shao-pan was branded a great-Han chauvinist, local nationalism was the accusation hurled at another Kwangsi "rightist," Huang Hsien-fan. Both views were said to be equally hostile to the full implementation in China of Marxist-Leninist theory on the national question.[19] Specifically, Huang Hsien-fan was said to have encouraged Chuang separatism with the idea of setting up an "independent kingdom" in western Kwangsi. He was also charged with having written a *Short History of the Kwangsi Chuang People* in which he minimized the role of the CCP in the Chuang uprisings of the late 1920's and blamed the Han Chinese nation, rather than one class within it, for the oppression which the Chuang people had long suffered in Kwangsi.[20] Basically, the "local nationalists" did not want Han cadres in Chuang areas, whereas the "Han chauvinists" did not want northerners in Kwangsi.[21]

A Preparatory Committee for the Kwangsi Chuang Autonomous Region, formed in September 1957,[22] was said by February 1958 to have completed its work of propaganda and indoctrination.[23] Meanwhile, a phonetic script had been developed for the Chuang language and published at the end of the year.[24] The Kwangsi Chuang Autonomous Region was formally established on March 5, 1958, by the first session of the First Kwangsi People's Congress, meeting at Nanning. The occasion was witnessed by dignitaries from Peking and other parts of China, as well as by a group of well-wishers from the Viet-Bac Thai autonomous area adjacent to Kwangsi. In an

[18] *Ibid.*, July 17, 1957.
[19] *Ibid.*, July 23, 1957.
[22] *Ibid.*, September 19, 1957.
[23] *Jen-min jih-pao*, February 10, 1958.
[24] *Kuang-hsi jih-pao*, January 22, 1958.

[20] *Ibid.*, September 1, 1957.
[21] *Ibid.*, December 22, 1957.

address to the gathering, the First Secretary of the Kwangsi CCP Committee appealed for unity among the various nationalities of the autonomous region.[25]

THE INTERIOR REGIONS OF YUNNAN

The establishment of national minority autonomous areas in the frontier regions of Yunnan, discussed in chapter 3, was followed by the establishment of similar autonomous areas in the interior. The frontier (*pien-chiang*) and interior (*nei-ti*) national minorities of Yunnan are treated as two distinct categories in the literature, reflecting the fact that they were dealt with separately in the implementation of actual policy. Thus, the *People's Daily*, in a despatch from Kunming on the last day of 1956, describes the situation as follows:

Yunnan has been carrying out the planned establishment of national minority autonomous areas since 1953. At present, the frontier regions [*pien-chiang ti-ch'ü*], excluding the K'awa area, which is still in a preparatory stage, but embracing all the places where the T'ai, Ching-p'o, Hani, Lisu, and Lahu are heavily represented, have all established autonomous *chou* or autonomous *hsien*. Beginning in 1956, the interior regions [*nei-ti*], too, in accordance with the wishes of the nationalities there, have established the Tali Pai Nationality Autonomous *Chou*, the Yung-chien Hui Nationality Autonomous *Hsien*, the Wei-shan Yi Nationality Autonomous *Hsien*, the Ning-lang Yi Nationality Autonomous *Hsien*, and the Kung-shan Tu-lung and Nu Nationality Autonomous *Hsien*.[26]

These were followed by the Lu-nan Yi Nationality Autonomous *Hsien* (late 1956), the Ti-ch'ing Tibetan Autonomous *Chou* (September 1957), the Li-chiang Na-hsi Autonomous *Hsien* (1958), and the Ch'u-hsiung Yi Autonomous *Chou* (1958). (The O-shan Yi Autonomous *Hsien* was an exceptional case, having been established in 1951.)

25 *Jen-min jih-pao*, March 14, 1958.
26 *Ibid.*, December 31, 1956.

AUTONOMOUS HSIEN AND AUTONOMOUS CHOU OF
YUNNAN PROVINCE (1963)
(Autonomous Chou in larger type.)

These three autonomous *chou* and seven autonomous *hsien*
in the interior, together with the five autonomous *chou* and
five autonomous *hsien* (one of which is still referred to as an
"area") on the frontier, brought Yunnan's total to eight autonomous *chou* and twelve autonomous *hsien* by the end of
1958:[27]

[27] Data presented in this table are based on contemporary reports
which appeared in the *People's Daily* and the *Yunnan Daily* during the
years 1956–1959.

Interior	Frontier
Ti-ch'ing Tibetan AC	Te-hung T'ai and Ching-p'o AC
Kung-shan Tu-lung and Nu AH	Keng-ma T'ai and K'awa AH
	Lan-tsang Lahu AH
Li-chiang Na-hsi AH	Meng-lien T'ai, Lahu, and K'awa AA
Tali Pai AC	
Yung-chien Hui AH	Hsi-shuang Pan-na T'ai AC
Wei-shan Yi AH	Chiang-ch'eng Hani and Yi AH
Ch'u-hsiung Yi AC	Hung-ho Hani and Yi AC
Lu-nan Yi AH	Wen-shan Chuang and Miao AC
O-shan Yi AH	Tsang-yuan K'awa AH
Ning-lang Yi AH	Nu-chiang Lisu AC

A 1965 listing from the *People's Handbook* (*Jen-min shou-ts'e*), which may be taken as more definitive, is presented as an appendix at the end of this study. There are only a few discrepancies between the two. With respect to the interior regions, the Yung-chien Hui AH and the Wei-shan Yi AH, contiguous areas lying within the Tali Pai AC, were later redefined as the Wei-shan Yi and Hui AH and the Nan-chien Yi AH. Otherwise, the designations of the interior areas were stable. With respect to the frontier regions, it will be noted that two national minority areas mentioned in chapter 3 are missing from the present list. These are the P'ing-pien Miao AH and the Ho-k'ou Yao AH, lying within the Hung-ho Hani and Yi AC. These two areas re-emerge in the 1965 listing. In addition, the formation of the Hsi-meng K'awa AH, still in preparation during 1956–1959, was completed by 1965.

There is a dearth of information concerning the establishment of national minority autonomous areas in the interior portions of Yunnan. Such information as we do have, however, indicates that the process in the interior was not very different from that on the frontier. The Ti-ch'ing Tibetan autonomous *chou* is a case in point. The three *hsien* comprising this *chou* sent delegates to an "all nationalities, all circles, people's representative congress" held at Chung-tien, the *chou*'s leading town, from September 6 to 13, 1957.[28] Of the 411 delegates, 211

[28] *Yün-nan jih-pao*, September 14, 1957.

were Tibetans; other nationalities represented were Na-hsi, Lisu, Pai, Yi, Hui, Nu, Hsi-fan, Han, and Miao. Also present were representatives of the Nationalities Affairs Commission of the CPG, the Yunnan Bureau of the CCP, and the Yunnan People's Council (represented by its Vice-chairman, Chang Chung). In addition, representatives came from various special districts and autonomous *chou* in Yunnan as well as from the adjacent provinces of Szechwan, Kweichow, and Kwangsi. The conference endorsed the following reports:

1. "Preparatory work carried out for [the establishment of] the autonomous *chou*";
2. "Accomplishments during the eight years since the liberation of the [area of the] Ti-ch'ing Tibetan autonomous *chou* and tasks for the future";
3. "The peaceful implementation of land reform in the fourth and fifth districts of Wei-hsi *hsien* and the Chin-sha district of Chung-tien *hsien*";
4. " (Draft) Regulations for the establishment of the People's Representative Congress and People's Council of the Ti-ch'ing autonomous *chou* of Yunnan province."

A Tibetan Chairman for the *chou*, together with several vice-chairmen of different nationalities, were elected, and the *chou* was formally established at a great meeting on the afternoon of September 13 attended by more than four thousand people.[29]

A similar pattern is evident in the establishment of the Ning-lang Yi autonomous *hsien*, one of three *hsien* comprising the Hsiao-liang-shan (Little Cold Mountains, as distinguished from the Great Cold Mountains [Ta-liang-shan] of Szechwan, also an Yi area) in northern Yunnan.[30] Although it was theoretically liberated in 1950, the first Chinese Communist work team did not penetrate the area until July 1953.[31] The Yi people here are pastoralists, depending on a cattle, sheep, and horse economy, in contrast to the Yi people

---

[29] *Ibid.*
[30] *Jen-min jih-pao*, October 6, 1958.
[31] *Yün-nan jih-pao*, August 27, 1953.

elsewhere in the province, who are predominantly agricul-turalists.[32]

Forty separate groups of Yi, along with Han, Miao, T'ai, Hui, Pai, Hani, Lisu, Chuang, and Yao, are said to inhabit the Chu-hsiung Yi autonomous *chou*, established on April 15, 1958. This is a large *chou* in the north-central part of the province. It contains 15 *hsien* and, at the time of its establishment, had a total population of 1.67 million, of which the Yi people comprised 23 percent. The area of the Chu-hsiung Yi autono-mous *chou*, which lies along the south bank of the Chin-hsia-chiang (River of Golden Sand, as the upper reaches of the Yangtze in Yunnan are called), was visited in 1935 by the Red Army during the Long March. Perhaps for this reason, the *chou*'s formative congress was attended by Hsieh Hou-ch'ou (a Chuang), Vice-chairman of the Nationalities Affairs Com-mission, and other senior CPG officials. Before liberation, slash-and-burn agriculture was practiced by some of the minorities here, a fact attributed to government oppression.[33]

There is nothing in the scattered information on the estab-lishment of other autonomous areas in the interior of Yun-nan[34] to indicate any marked divergence from the usual pattern. It would seem that the implementation of the Party's policy of regional autonomy for national minorities, carefully initiated in the politically sensitive frontier areas (where there was a correspondingly large use of united front tactics), was carried out methodically and without fanfare in the relatively secure interior.[35]

[32] *Ibid.*, September 28, 1954.

[33] *Jen-min jih-pao*, April 18, 1958.

[34] For example, the *Yün-nan jih-pao* of January 16 and September 25, 1957, on the Lu-nan Yi autonomous *hsien*; the *Kwang-ming jih-pao* of De-cember 14, 1956, on the Wei-shan Yi autonomous *hsien* and the Yung-chien Hui autonomous *hsien*.

[35] As an instance of this dichotomy, it is noteworthy that the Kung-shan Tu-lung and Nu autonomous *hsien* is considered an interior area despite the fact that it is physically situated on the frontier. Presumably, this is because the *hsien* is administratively within the Nu-chiang Lisu autonomous *chou* and therefore regarded as sort of an "out-back" of the *chou*.

There is a certain lack of consistency about the term "frontier" in the literature we have been considering. In general, and this agrees with our usage here, the term refers to those areas situated on the border with Burma and Laos, but sometimes areas adjacent to Vietnam are included. This seems to have been more the case before 1954 than after, suggesting that the elimination of hostile forces from North Vietnam, resulting from the Viet Minh victory and the Geneva settlement, did away, at least temporarily, with the "frontier" character of the Sino-Vietnamese border.[36] Data concerning the Hung-ho Hani autonomous area and the Wen-shan Chuang and Miao autonomous area are illustrative of this change.

The Wen-shan Chuang and Miao autonomous *chou*, established in 1958, is not usually referred to as a frontier area, although it is situated in the angle formed by the Yunnan-Vietnam and Yunnan-Kwangsi borders. The non-Han peoples of the Wen-shan Chuang and Miao autonomous *chou* are more akin to those of Kwangsi than to those of the rest of Yunnan, and its formation was imitative of the West Kwangsi autonomous *chou*, established in 1956. Immediately following the creation of a preparatory committee for the Wen-shan Chuang and Miao autonomous *chou*, a 134-man delegation, led by a Chuang, was sent, by road via Pai-se, to Nanning to study the organization of the West Kwangsi Chuang autonomous *chou*. The group stayed in Kwangsi for more than a month during the spring of 1957.[37] The Wen-shan Chuang and Miao autonomous *chou* covered the same area as Wen-shan special district (Wen-shan *chuan-ch'ü*), which it superseded in 1958. The various nationalities in the *chou* comprised just over half of the area's total population of 1.4 million; the remainder were Han Chinese. However, the ethnic make-up of the area was so

[36] Traditionally, the Yunnan-Tibet border also came under the category of frontier territory. In early Chinese Communist literature this designation is applied to Li-chiang special district, adjacent to Sikang ("inner" Tibet). Probably this usage reflected a strong provincial orientation on the part of the Yunnan CCP committee as well as a residual feeling that the Tibetan highlands were somehow "foreign." As autonomous areas were established in northern Yunnan, however, the term "frontier" gradually ceased being applied to this area.

[37] *Kuang-hsi jih-pao*, April 17, 1957.

complex that investigation into the identity of some of the groups was still proceeding at the time the preparatory committee for the *chou* was set up.[38]

The Hung-ho Hani autonomous area, usually considered a part of the Yunnanese frontier, seems to have lost much of its frontier character when it was enlarged in 1957 by the addition of "interior" territory, thereby more than doubling its size. This occurred as the area was raised to the status of a *chou*. The Hung-ho Hani autonomous area had been carved out of Meng-tze special district in 1954 (see chapter 3); now its area of four *hsien* was rejoined with Meng-tze's eight *hsien* to form the Hung-ho Hani and Yi autonomous *chou*.[39] The new territory lies on the north bank of the Red River and is largely (outside the towns) Yi in population, whereas the old area was limited to the south bank of the Red River, occupying the space between the river and the Vietnamese frontier. The Hani, an industrious people who terraced the hillsides for paddy fields, now comprise only 18 percent of the population, as compared with 26 percent for the Yi and 40.6 percent for the Han. The decision to establish the Hung-ho Hani and Yi autonomous *chou* was said to have been made by a joint meeting of the Meng-tze and Hung-ho people's congresses held in July 1957, confirmed by the State Council in September, and ratified by the first session of the first people's congress of the new *chou*. The keynote speech at the latter occasion was delivered by Huang T'ien-ming, first secretary of the Meng-tze CCP bureau; his topic was "Prepare to thoroughly promote socialist education and raise the enthusiasm of the *chou*'s masses for the production high tide."[40] Perhaps the most noteworthy feature of the separate development of the Hung-ho Hani autonomous area and Meng-tze special district is that, in the former, land reform of the "peaceful, consultative" form was carried out, whereas in the latter the Yi people experienced regular land reform along with the Han Chinese. By the time the preparatory committee for the Hung-ho Hani and

[38] *Jen-min jih-pao*, April 10, 1957.
[39] *Ibid.*, November 20, 1957.
[40] *Yün-nan jih-pao*, November 14, 1957.

Yi autonomous *chou* was formed in July 1957, the Yi had completed both land reform and agricultural cooperativization, while the Hani, having accomplished the less rigorous type of land reform, were just beginning to form agricultural mutual-aid teams (the lower stage of "socialist transformation").[41]

The lack of detailed information on the establishment of autonomous areas in the interior of Yunnan, as compared with those on the frontier, undoubtedly reflects the shift in national priorities that had occurred by 1956. Minority policy was being superseded, as a fundamental national issue, by such concerns as implementation of the First Five-year Plan and the cooperative movement in agriculture. This trend was reinforced by the cooling in Sino-Soviet relations, which can be traced back to the Twentieth Party Congress of the Soviet Union (February 1956); the number of Soviet and Czech ethnographers visiting Yunnan fell off rapidly after 1956. The subsequent Sinification of Communist policy in China made itself felt in national minority affairs during 1956 in the form of a thoroughgoing policy review. This coincided with the Hundred Flowers campaign and culminated in the struggle against "local nationalism" which unfolded during 1957.

The review of national minority policy in Yunnan is considered here because it was carried out in the second half of 1956 and early 1957, at the same time that the bulk of the autonomous areas in the interior were being formed. In fact, under the slogan of *i-pien chien-ch'a, i-pien kai-chin* (at the same time investigate [the policy] and advance [our work]), the two became closely intertwined.[42] The same effort received scant attention in Kwangsi where, as we have seen, the Party's concern with the Cantonese population overshadowed the national minority problem. It is to be observed, however, that in both provinces CCP organizations at the local level were still being formed at this time;[43] their formation was related to the

[41] *Ibid.*, July 16, 1957.

[42] *Ibid.*, February 20, 1957. It was anticipated at the time the policy review was initiated that regional autonomy would be fully implemented in Yunnan before the end of 1957; see *Yün-nan jih-pao*, July 9, 1956.

[43] An editorial in the *Yunnan Daily* of December 11, 1956 exhorted

convening in June 1956 of the first congresses of the provincial
CCP committees of Yunnan and Kwangsi, which, in turn, an-
ticipated the Eighth National CCP Congress held in Peking in
September 1956.

The investigation of national minority policy in Yunnan
was carried out under direct CCP supervision. It utilized local
government organizations and the PLA in addition to the
Party apparatus.[44] The investigation was formally initiated by
the first Yunnan CCP congress, although it appears to have
actually started by late May.[45] Its objective was to assess the
Party's nationalities work of the preceding six years and to set
guidelines for further efforts in the same field.[46] A basic contention of the Yunnan CCP committee was, reportedly, that
the nationalities problem had advanced to a new stage—from
the stage of democratic reform (centering on land reform) to
the stage of socialist transformation (centering on the establishment of agricultural cooperatives).[47] As this was an axial
concept in the deliberations of the Eighth National CCP Congress, there is no reason to doubt that the investigation work
in Yunnan was ordered by higher Party echelons.

The following assessment of the national minority problem
was said to have been made by the June congress of the Yunnan CCP committee:[48]

> Owing to the correct implementation of central [*chung-yang*]
> plans, policies, and directives on the part of the provincial
> committee and organizations at various levels, the Party has
> been enabled to score important victories with respect to na-
> tionalities work. At present, among agricultural villages in
> the interior which have completed land reform, there are
> four million dispersed or concentrated peoples of the national
> minorities, and these have already basically gone through
> semi-socialist cooperativization, with 30 percent of the house-

the Party to work harder in establishing local-level Party organizations in
national minority areas.

[44] *Yün-nan jih-pao*, February 21, 1957.

[45] *Ibid.*, September 6, 1956 (editorial).

[46] *Yün-nan jih-pao*, July 9, 1956.

[47] *Jen-min jih-pao*, June 7, 1956.

[48] *Ibid.*, July 9, 1956.

holds having joined the superior level agricultural producers cooperatives [collective farms]. In areas where the frontier minorities are concentrated, areas accounting for 800,000 people have already completed land reform by means of the peaceful, consultative form and have, moreover, established more than 1,000 pivotal producers' cooperatives. Furthermore, [land] reform will be completed this year in the Hsi-shuang pan-na T'ai nationality autonomous *chou* and the Hung-ho Hani nationality autonomous area [*chou*]. And social experimentation is being undertaken among the Lisu and Ching-p'o, who have no clear class distinctions. The congress declared that each nationality's socialist transformation and socialist construction constitutes the new content of the nationalities question [in Yunnan].

After pointing out that the way in which each nationality entered socialism would have to depend on the special characteristics of that nationality, the congress proceeded to categorize Yunnan's non-Han people into four groups:

1. The three million national minority people who live in level or hilly areas, among whom agricultural cooperativization can proceed at the same pace as in Han areas.

2. The one million national minority people who live in high, cold, mountainous areas and who need special help because of the difficult conditions of their lives.

3. The frontier nationalities who have already completed land reform and among whom cooperatives may be gradually and carefully established.[49]

4. The nearly 700,000 Ching-p'o, Lisu, and K'awa (frontier uplanders) who should receive state assistance so as to develop their economic and cultural base.

This categorization brings into focus the real dynamics of the national minority situation in Yunnan. The dwellers of the interior lowlands (first category), comprising half of the province's total national minority population, are to be handled in much the same way as the Han Chinese, from whom they are only incidentally distinguishable. The Yi and the Pai

[49] Of a frontier lowland population of approximately 1.5 million, 600,000 had completed land reform by June 1956: *Yün-nan jih-pao*, June 22, 1956.

are the most numerous groups in this category. Special handling is required for the mountain dwellers of the second category, who are predominantly alpine pastoralists. The frontier lowlanders of the third category, among whom the T'ai constitute the largest group, are singled out for attention not because of any distinctive pattern of livelihood but rather on account of their exposed position on the frontier. The fourth category comprises the hill dwellers of the frontier, who have both a distinctive way of life (notably slash-and-burn agriculture) and access to the outside. Clearly, the geographical position of Yunnan's minority groups with respect to altitude (upland/lowland) and to the frontier (interior/exterior) were weighty determinants of national minority policy in the view of the Yunnan CCP Committee; correspondingly less importance was attached to the various autonomous areas as distinctive units. As has already been indicated, the dichotomy interior/exterior was manifested in the priority given the frontier groups in the implementation of regional autonomy; operationally, the special treatment accorded frontier groups took concrete form in the "peaceful, consultative method of land reform" (*ho-ping hsieh-shang t'u-ti kai-ke ti fang-shih*).[50] The dichotomy upland/lowland made itself felt during the 1956/57 investigation of national minority policy, when it was found that there were serious shortcomings in the Party's work among those nationalities whose mode of life was fundamentally different from that of the Han Chinese. To meet this situation, the Yunnan CCP committee called upon all appropriate *hsien* to set up "work committees for mountainous areas" (*shan-ch'ü kung-tso wei-yüan-hui*), which would penetrate the mountain regions in order "to understand the needs and sufferings of the people there."[51] Thus, as in Kwangsi, the autonomous units established under the Party's national minor-

[50] Reference was made to this fact in an important speech by the First Secretary of the Yunnan CCP committee, Hsieh Fu-ch'ih, to the Eighth National CCP Congress entitled, "On the basis of national characteristics separately lead the national minorities to socialism" (Ken-chü min-tsu t'e-tien fen-pieh yin-tao shao-shu mih-tsu tsou hsiang she-hui chu-i), *Yün-nan jih-pao*, October 1, 1956.

[51] *Yün-nan jih-pao*, February 20, 1957.

ity policy did not provide a sufficient basis for the implementation of subsequent nationalities policy, for they coincided only
imperfectly with the political realities with which the provincial CCP committee had to deal.

The more than ten nationalities (never specified) inhabiting
Yunnan's mountainous regions lived in some one thousand
scattered villages.[52] Estimates of the national minority population of the interior mountains jumped by 25 per cent in the
course of the investigation effort of 1956. The figure in July
was an even one million, which must have been a very rough
calculation.[53] In October, it was said that the total population
of the interior mountain regions was 1.6 million, of which
eighty percent, or 1.28 million, were people of the national
minorities (the remainder being Han Chinese).[54] The political
problem posed by these people will be briefly sketched here,
and the frontier question will be the subject of the next
chapter.

The term "mountain regions" (shan ch'ü) is not given precise definition in the literature on the subject. Indeed, the
vagueness of the term suggests that the Party itself did not
know exactly what the term implied, leading one to suspect
that lurking here is a very traditional Han Chinese notion of
faraway places inhabited by strange people. Awe is mixed with
condescension in the longer term commonly employed, "high,
cold, and desolate mountain regions" (kao han p'in-chi shan-
ch'ü), and the most talked-about aspect of the people living
there is their poverty and backwardness. In tones reminiscent
of American descriptions of "underdeveloped countries," attention is focused on the low per capita income of the mountain people, said to average twenty yüan per year,[55] as an indi-
cation of their disadvantaged position. One's suspicion that
"mountain regions" has a beyond-the-pale connotation is
strengthened by the accusation of "great-Han chauvinist thinking" (ta-han-tsu chu-i szu-hsiang) on the part of cadres involved

52 Ibid., October 9, 1956.
53 Ibid., July 19, 1956.
54 Ibid., October 9, 1956. It is well known that no direct count of the
population of outlying regions was made for the 1953 census.
55 Ibid., October 9, 1956.

in—or, frequently, neglecting—work with the mountain people. This charge was made at a special work conference on
mountain regions which met from September 24 to 30, 1956,
under the auspices of the Yunnan provincial CCP committee.
Attacking great-Han chauvinism, it said, was essential if the
campaign against subjectivism and bureaucratism in mountain work was to succeed.[56] The conference emphasized the
importance of investigating more thoroughly the situation of
the national minorities in mountainous regions and, repeating
an ultimatum issued by the Yunnan CCP committee in June,
called upon the relevant local and *hsien* committees (*k'e ti,
hsien wei*) to speedily organize work committees for the mountain regions.[57]

The formula for "transforming the backward face of the
mountain districts" was "one small [*i shao*], two big [*erh to*],
and three honest [*san kung tao*]," interpreted as, first, ask for
little (*yao ti shao*), second, give a lot (*kei ti to*), and, third, fair
price [equitable value in exchange transactions] (*wu-chia kung
tao*). In explaining the importance of this formula, a *Yunnan
Daily* editorial in July had pointed out that the mountain
peoples were still not being treated justly, and that, therefore,
their poverty could not be explained entirely as a product of
history. It complained that the special features, and especially
the impoverished condition, of the local population had not
been heeded by financial and economic ministry branches in
carrying out their functions in mountain regions. Because the
trade bureau organs (*shang-yeh pu-men*) had not succeeded in
penetrating deeply into the remote mountain regions (the im-
plication is that private traders in the past had indeed done so),
the national minorities had not been able to purchase daily
necessities nor to sell their local products. This had adversely
affected the food situation, so that in Yung-shan *hsien*, for example, investigation showed that, on account of bureaucratic
policy of "taking much [grain] and leaving little," the hill peo-

[56] *Jen-min jih-pao*, October 9, 1956.

[57] *Ibid.* During the contemporary rectification campaign, the normal
punishment for Party members being dsiciplined was to be "sent down
[to the country]" (*hsia-fang*), but in Yunnan this frequently took the form
of being sent "up to the mountains" (*shang-shan*).

ple had only potatoes to eat for seven or eight months of the year.[58] The bigger the harvest, the bigger the requisitions. Instances had occurred of people of the national minorities, driven by the needs of sickness or of young children, traveling 300 li without being able to buy grain to eat. The editorial concluded, needless to say, that the masses in the mountainous regions were not content.[59]

Commenting on the results of the mountain region work conference and the Party's experience in working with the upland minority peoples over the preceding years, a Yunnan Daily editorial of October 1956[60] pointed out that there was a fundamental contradiction (mao-tun) between the backwardness of these peoples and their advance toward socialism. It was imperative that the efficiency of their mixed economy, embracing forestry, herding, and agriculture, be increased. In general, however, the national minorities lacked initiative, while the overweening attitude and ignorance of local conditions exhibited by Han cadres prevented them from being very effective. The editorial contended that Han cadres must be purged of chauvinistic attitudes, whereas national minority cadres were encouraged to adopt a more positive attitude. Party, as well as government, cadres from the national minorities must be trained. All of these approaches should be furthered as the state moves to improve the health and educational facilities available to the hill people. Nowhere, however, was the Party's policy of regional autonomy even mentioned in this discussion, even though the editorial appeared at the very time that the policy was being extended to the interior regions of the province. Evidently it was not felt that regional autonomy was particularly relevant to the political problems posed by the upland minority peoples of Yunnan.

[58] Interestingly, Yung-shan does not lie within a formally constituted national minority autonomous area. It is situated in northern Yunnan, across the Chin-sha-chiang from the Ta-liang-shan region of Szechwan. Yung-shan hsien has a large Yi population, interspersed with Miao. Obviously, "mountain regions," and the problems associated with them, are not limited to autonomous areas.

[59] Yün-nan jih-pao, July 19, 1956.

[60] Ibid., October 9, 1956.

5

THE TRANSFORMATION OF THE YUNNAN FRONTIER

A REVIEW of developments on the frontier of Yunnan (subsequent to the establishment of autonomous areas there) may conveniently begin by considering a 1956 frontier work conference called by the provincial CCP committee. Like the mountain region work conference considered in the previous chapter, this frontier work conference was convened following the conclusion of the Eighth National Congress of the CCP.[1] Beginning November 6 and ending on November 17, the frontier work conference was attended by more than one hundred leading and basic level cadres from the various administrative units on the frontier, including the Te-hung T'ai and Ching-p'o autonomous *chou*, the Hsi-shuang Pan-na

---

[1] The relative importance of the two is perhaps suggested by the fact that the frontier work conference lasted nearly twice as long (eleven days compared to six days) as the mountain region work conference.

T'ai autonomous *chou*, the Hung-ho Hani and Yi autonomous *chou*, and the Nu-chiang Lisu autonomous *chou*.[2]

The two main tasks for the conference were to summarize the results of land reform and to discuss problems of developing production and cooperativization. Regarding accomplishments to date in frontier areas, it was noted that the policy of "peaceful, consultative, land reform" (*ho-p'ing ts'an-shang t'u-kai*) had been realized and that nearly one thousand agricultural cooperatives had been tested. As a result, there had been great changes on the frontier with respect to political, economic, and cultural affairs; the transformation of class and nationality relationships was particularly noted. The conference maintained that the urgent demand of all the frontier nationalities at present was to move forward in expanding production, to progressively transform (*kai-pien*) each nationality's backward appearance, and to steadily improve the material and cultural well-being of the people. For historical reasons, however, the social productivity of the people in this area was very low; therefore, according to the same report, socialist cooperativization must be based on the unique characteristics of each people. It was also noted that there was very little experience in carrying out the cooperative movement in frontier areas and that experience from interior regions could not be blindly applied. Moreover, the pace of cooperativization in the frontier regions could not be too rapid: it would be enough if only five percent of the planned cooperativization of the frontier area was attained in the first year.

It was pointed out that experience with the nearly one thousand experimental cooperatives had shown that in order to increase production on the frontier it was not enough to expand agriculture alone: side industries (*fu-yeh*) and handicrafts should also be expanded. Moreover, the output of commercial crops should be expanded along with the output of food crops, and individual needy families had to be helped at the same time that cooperatives were being promoted. After thoroughly analyzing cadre working style in frontier areas, the

2 *Jen-min jih-pao*, November 20, 1956.

conference applauded the close relationship which local cadres of the national minorities and outside Han cadres, working together, had formed with the common people. Without such a relationship, the results to that date in frontier work could not have been achieved. For the future, Han cadres should always try to defer to the sensibilities of nationality cadres, lest they fall into great-Han chauvinist ways. At the same time, Han cadres should try to stimulate a positive spirit on the part of their national minority colleagues. Finally, the conference referred to Chairman Mao's warning against chauvinistic tendencies (*ta-kuo chu-i ch'ing-hsiang*) in its consideration of the ties between frontier regions and the exterior (*pien-chiang ti-ch'ü tui wai kuan-hsi*).[3]

The *Yunnan Daily*'s coverage of the frontier work conference included significant details not touched upon in the story carried by the *People's Daily*.[4] It observed that the conference participants had studied the documents of the Eighth National CCP Congress prior to attending the conference. It left no doubt that there was more than coincidence in the appearance among the frontier minorities of enthusiasm for cooperatives and the endorsement of the cooperative movement by the Eighth National Congress. It did, however, advance a theoretical justification for this enthusiasm: namely, the contention that the land reform movement, thus far applied to frontier areas with a population of 1.4 million (i.e., excluding the hill peoples), had broken up the system of feudal tenure, thereby setting free the productive power of the agricultural villages.

A contradiction remained, however, between the productive forces liberated from feudalism and the frontier's social backwardness left over from history. The conference declared that the various nationalities must be led by the CCP to increase pro-

[3] *Ibid.* The epochal meeting of Prime Ministers U Nu and Chou En-lai was held in mid-December 1956 at the frontier town of Mang-shih. It will be considered later in the context of trans-frontier relations.

[4] *Yün-nan jih-pao*, November 27, 1956. The issue carried an editorial as well as a news item dealing with the conference; both appeared on the front page. The *People's Daily* coverage had appeared a week earlier, on the final day of the conference (November 20).

duction, which would create a favorable climate for the cooperative movement.[5] According to the *Yunnan Daily*, the one thousand experimental cooperatives formed on the frontier in the spring of 1956 had all reported increased production. To the extent that these cooperatives were to have produced theory and method specifically applicable to frontier minority areas, however, the experiment had been a failure, for in building these cooperatives, experience had simply been transferred from the Yunnanese interior. Therefore, further testing was necessary. Evidence of the failure could be found in the attitude of the farmers themselves, who had simply gone along with the cooperatives without understanding the implications of socialist production. Blame for the weakness of the cooperative movement on the frontier was placed squarely on the higher echelon cadres (*ling-tao kan-pu*), who were predominantly Han Chinese. It was said that in their subjectivist attempt to get quick results, these leading Han cadres all but ignored the frontier question and the national minority question.[6]

Before proceeding to a review of developments in specific autonomous areas, the very large role which the PLA played on the frontier ought to be underscored. Not only, as we have seen, was the Army Peking's instrument for the liberation of the frontier, but it also bore the responsibility of inducing loyalty to the new regime on the part of the minorities whilst the Party and Government apparatus was being organized for frontier work in Yunnan. In the lowland, mainly T'ai areas, the delay was comparatively short, but in more remote hill areas, such as the K'awa mountains, the importance of the military tended to persist. For longer or shorter periods throughout the frontier areas, then, the PLA carried the weight of the national minority policy of the PRC. Some of the techniques used by the PLA in this work, especially during the period between the formal end of "pacification" (and the promulgation

[5] "*Ch'üan-mien ling-tao pien-chiang ti-ch'ü fa-chan sheng-ch'an: shen wei chao-k'ai pien-chiang t'u-kai ch'ü nung-yeh ho-tso-hua hui-i tso le yen-chiu,*" *Yün-nan jih-pao*, November 27, 1956.

[6] *Yün-nan jih-pao*, November 27, 1956, editorial.

of the *General Program*) in 1952 and the establishment of autonomous areas in 1953, 1954, and later, will be briefly reviewed here.

The *People's Daily* reported in June 1952 that the PLA on the frontier, thanks to the help it had rendered the national minorities, had earned the title of "the great happiness troops [*hung-fu pu-tui*] sent by Chairman Mao." In addition to chasing bandits, they were credited with having given the people clothing and food, and especially salt. They had improved fresh water supplies for the hill people and helped them improve their farming technique.[7] The PLA was joined by peripatetic "frontier work cadres" (*pien-chiang-ch'ü kung-tso ti kan-pu*) sent from the interior; together they initiated a "good deeds program" (*tso hao shih yün-tung*).[8] The frontier minorities were said to have gladly reciprocated by forming labor battalions (*min-kung-tui*) for the construction of roads. The following is one of the ditties they reportedly sang while at work:

> We build roads on the frontier of the motherland,
> Uniting together we shall certainly win,
> Overcoming difficulties we can transform the earth,
> Open the mountain roads, open the mountain roads,
> Put through highways to guard the frontiers![9]

Especially during 1953, the *Yunnan Daily* ran a series of "frontier reports" (*pien-chiang t'ung-hsin*) in which individual participants in border work reminisced about their experiences, always triumphant.[10] One of these stated that a fighting force (*i ko chan-t'ou tui*) was always, in addition, a work force (*i ko kung-tso tui*), and that irrigation ditches had high priority among the various projects.[11] We learn from another that security troops (*kung-an pu-tui*) were active on the frontier along with the Army.[12] In one "frontier report," we are in-

[7] *Jen-min jih-pao*, August 14, 1952.
[8] *Yün-nan jih-pao*, October 1, 1952.
[9] *Ibid.*, April 19, 1953.
[10] I have located and studied several dozen of these, the earliest dated January 23, 1953 and the last May 11, 1955.
[11] April 16, 1953.
[12] April 28, 1953.

formed that it was only in 1953 that the government sent a nationalities work team to the outpost at Man-sa in the Ying River area of the Te-hung T'ai and Ching-p'o autonomous area.[13] With reference to the same area, another report tells us that Han Chinese were not initially welcomed by the Ching-p'o there, but that gradually the native people became convinced that Chinese Communists were more trustworthy than the Chiang Kai-shek bandits who had operated there in the past.[14]

Elsewhere, we are told that the PLA frontier troops operated mobile dispensaries as part of a "patriotic health movement" (ai-kuo wei-sheng yün-tung)[15] and helped the national minorities establish auxiliary defense forces (lien fang tui)[16] as well as their own militia (min-ping).[17] Some national minority individuals joined the PLA itself.[18]

Further details concerning the results of the PLA's work with the frontier minorities appeared in the Peking paper, China Youth, which sought to attract young Han Chinese to patriotic projects such as developing the frontier regions of the country. In August 1956 it carried a story entitled "Unite [with] the fraternal nationalities, build up the frontiers of the motherland—implementation of nationalities policy by the PLA in Yunnan bears fruit."[19] One of the things the Army had accomplished during the preceding four years in one area, according to the report, was to help the fraternal nationalities build or repair more than 500 kilometers of post roads (i tao) and more than 200 bridges, thereby linking together more than 200 large and small villages and outposts centered on Meng-la Pan-na, on the Lao border. The people's livelihood had improved greatly in the same area, thanks to the develop-

---

[13] July 4, 1954.

[14] April 12, 1954.

[15] Yün-nan jih-pao, March 6, 1954.

[16] Ibid., September 30, 1954.

[17] Ibid., October 19, 1954.

[18] Ibid., October 3, 1956.

[19] "T'uan-chieh hsiung-ti min-tsu, chien-she tsu-kuo pien-chiang—yün-nan ti chieh-fang chün chih-hsing min-tsu cheng-ts'e yu ch'eng-chi," Chung-kuo ch'ing-nien pao, August 23, 1956.

ment of trade. Treatment had been given to 18,000 people
suffering from various illnesses; communicable diseases had
been virtually stamped out, and the national minorities had
been assisted in making their living conditions more hygienic.
Moreover, the local government had been helped by the Army
to open schools and expand literacy. Thanks to these efforts,
the story concluded, the masses of the people had been brought
into the struggle against the enemy. "Once, when a band of
Chiang bandits crossed the frontier, the local people came in
the middle of the night to report it, enabling our troops to
destroy the intruders. On another occasion, the warning of a
T'ai compatriot enabled us to quickly apprehend and send
back some agents (*t'e-wu fen-tzu*) who had escaped from a Vietnamese prison."[20]

Six months later the same paper reported that frontier security forces (*pien-fang pu-tui*) had called a meeting to discuss
results and shortcomings in national minority work during the
previous two years.[21] These forces, according to the report, had
helped different nationalities establish 491 mutual-aid teams
and 73 agricultural cooperatives, set up 73 night schools and
24 day schools, spread common-sense knowledge about hygiene, and given medical attention to nearly a million persons.
Under party and government control, moreover, these forces
had fostered positive elements (*chi-chi fen-tzu*) and expanded
party membership.[22] The slogan for the PLA's thirtieth anniversary celebrations held in outlying regions of Yunnan on
August 1, 1957, was "Strengthen army-people unity, safeguard
the country's frontiers!" (*Chia-chiang chün min t'uan-chieh,
kung-ku tzu-kuo pien-chiang*).[23]

Perhaps the most spectacular change on the Yunnanese
frontier was the reduction of malaria to manageable proportions. It was mainly the PLA which carried out this task. The
eradication of the anopheles mosquito was as much the objective of the campaign against malaria as was the treatment of

[20] *Ibid.*
[21] *Chung-kuo ch'ing-nien pao*, March 2, 1957.
[22] *Ibid.*
[23] *Yün-nan jih-pao*, August 3, 1957.

victims of the disease. Thus, drainage and sanitation work was an important part of the campaign. By 1956 the death rate from the disease had fallen to 0.196 percent, compared with 0.419 percent in 1953. Moreover, whereas malaria had been common in pre-liberation days, by 1956 only one percent of the population was infected. When the campaign began in 1950, the PLA, backed by various ministries, established thirteen malaria prevention stations and organized a number of mobile teams to fight the anopheles mosquito. Thus, the population of Szemao, which by 1950 had fallen to 1,000 from a level of 50,000 prior to an epidemic which began in 1919, had risen to 4,000 by 1958. A similar pattern was observable throughout the tropical belt of southern Yunnan, extending from Mang-shih in the Te-hung T'ai and Ching-p'o autonomous *chou* to the lower reaches of the Mekong River in the Hsi-shuang pan-na T'ai autonomous *chou* and even to the Hung-ho *chou*. By the beginning of 1958 the PLA was said to have covered 50,000 square kilometers in its struggle against malaria, which was directly assisted by the patriotic hygiene movement (*ai-kuo wei-sheng yün-tung*) already referred to.[24] With the eradication of malaria, there fell an age-old barrier to Han Chinese expansion in the frontier regions of Yunnan.

CADRES

As autonomous areas on the frontier of Yunnan came into being, the role of the PLA in national minority work was gradually reduced. Party and government organizations in the newly established autonomous areas now had to be greatly strengthened. A key requisite for this transition was the training of national minority cadres. This enterprise also served the objective of "nationalizing" (*min-tsu hua*) the administrative organizations of the autonomous areas and giving substance to the slogan of "home rule" (*tang-chia tso-chu*) for the national minorities. Initially, Han Chinese provided the main

[24] *Pien-chiang ch'ing-nien pao* (Kunming), January 25, 1958. Farther down the Mekong, in Laos, the UN's World Health Organization was fighting the battle against malaria, as personally observed by the present writer.

force for the autonomous area governments, which in many cases were merely headed by traditional leaders of the national minorities, won over to the new regime through the efforts of the CCP's United Front Work Department.

Coordination for the training of national minority cadres in Yunnan was provided by the provincial Nationalities Institute (min-tsu hsüeh-yüan) established at Kunming on August 1, 1951.[25] Its activities were much publicized, and it became a Mecca for foreign visitors, especially Soviet bloc ethnographers. The Institute's first class, of nearly 400 national minority cadres, was graduated in April 1952.[26] The second class to pass through the Institute numbered about 600, and the third class, which began in May 1953, passed the 800 mark.[27] During these years, the composition of the student body underwent a change, from one with a majority of students from interior parts of the province to one in which students from frontier regions predominated.[28] Many of the latter had achieved notoriety as model laborers or milita heroes, whereas membership in the New China Youth League had been enough to recommend students for the earlier classes.[29] Given this stimulus, the number of national minority cadres in the four frontier autonomous *chou* of Nu-chiang, Te-hung, Hsi-shuang Pan-na, and Hung-ho rose to 2,200, or thirty percent of the total in those areas, by 1955.[30] Within these frontier areas, the proportion of nationality cadres to the total number of cadres varied considerably: in the Hsi-shuang Pan-na it was sixty percent,[31] but in the Te-hung *chou* it was only sixteen percent.[32]

In addition to the Nationalities Institute in Kunming, Yunnan was served by two higher-echelon institutes. Senior officials from Yunnan's national minority regions, such as chair-

25 *Yün-nan jih-pao*, September 3, 1951. August 1 is Red Army Day.
26 *Ibid.*, April 8, 1952.
27 *Ibid.*, May 5, 1953.
28 *Ibid.*, September 28, 1954.
29 *Ibid.*, May 5, 1953.
30 *Kuang-ming jih-pao*, March 2, 1955.
31 *Jen-min jih-pao*, April 19, 1956.
32 *Ibid.*, July 14, 1957.

men of *hsien* people's governments, attended the Nationalities
Institute in Peking or the regional Nationalities Institute for
southwest China, located in Chengtu (Szechwan). By the end
of 1956, over 6,000 national minority cadres for Yunnan had
been trained at these three schools. After graduation, they returned to work in their own areas.[33] Low-level cadres, meanwhile, were receiving training at the sub-provincial level—that
is, without going to Kunming. It appears that more than twice
as many national minority cadres were trained at special-
district capitals (e.g., Pao-shan, Meng-tse), or in their own autonomous areas, as were sent to the provincial capital and
beyond. The total for all national minority cadres from Yunnan trained by early 1956 was 17,000 or fifteen percent of the
total number of cadres in the province.[34] Despite the dramatic
growth in the number of national minority cadres, therefore,
Han Chinese were still expected to play an important role in
developing Yunnan's autonomous regions. As a cadre of the
Ai-ni nationality from the Hsi-shuang Pan-na T'ai autonomous *chou* put it, "The help of Han cadres is essential if the
frontier nationalities, with their backward economy and culture, are to develop into modern socialist nationalities."[35] Beginning in 1953, the Nationalities Affairs Committee of the
Yunnan People's Government provided a subsidy to autonomous area governments for the support of Han cadres working
on the frontier.[36]

The role of the provincial Nationalities Institute, and the
relevance of the Party's own national-minority policy, came
into serious question in 1957, as the nationwide anti-rightist
campaign rolled over Yunnan. In the course of this campaign,
the old guard in Yunnan, headed by Lung Yün (of Yi ancestry), was driven from power. One of his proteges was Ma
Shou-hsien (a Moslem), a key man in the Nationalities Institute in Kunming. Ma and his friends were accused of raising
national banners in opposition to ccp leadership and of scheming to return to reactionary leadership. The anti-rightist strug-

[33] *Yün-nan jih-pao,* May 7, 1957.   [35] *Ibid.,* December 11, 1956.
[34] *Ibid.,* April 17, 1956.   [36] *Ibid.,* May 18, 1954.

gle was carried out "in every corner of the Institute," with all the students participating. They wrote slogans and prepared posters in their own languages, all of which proclaimed their support of the CCP and of socialism; their determination to complete the social and national transformation of frontier, mountain, and interior minorities; and their repudiation of the "criminal words and deeds" of the anti-Party rightists. It was said that the rightists and their accomplices had even resorted to murder, presumably of Han cadres working in remote areas, and that "the bleached bones of persons slaughtered during the year could still be seen in the Nu-chiang Lisu autonomous *chou*." [37]

THE T'AI REGIONS OF YUNNAN

Certain aspects of the transformation of the Yunnanese frontier will now be considered with special reference to the Te-hung T'ai and Ching-p'o autonomous *chou* and the Hsi-shuang Pan-na T'ai autonomous *chou*, which together account for two-thirds of Yunnan's half-million T'ai population. These areas, more than any others on the southern frontier of the People's Republic of China, exhibited the dynamics of strong trans-frontier relations—based on ethnic, linguistic, religious, and historical ties—at the time of their liberation in 1949. The political process leading up to the establishment of these two autonomous *chou* was traced in chapter 3. Originally established as autonomous areas (*ch'ü*), they were redesignated as *chou* when the PRC state Constitution came into effect in early 1955.[38] The content of regional autonomy in these *chou* and its impact on the people there will now be reviewed, following which I shall return to discussion of frontier problems in general.

A degree of autonomy was nothing new for the frontier T'ai of Yunnan, who had long enjoyed self-government under loose supervision from Kunming and Peking. The PRC, apparently in recognition of this circumstance, presented seals (*yin-hsin*)

[37] *Ibid.*, September 15, 1957.
[38] *Kuang-ming jih-pao*, June 18, 1955.

of office to the T'ai princely rulers of the Hsi-shuang Pan-na and Te-hung autonomous *chou*. The presentations were made in ceremonies held at Kunming approximately six months following the establishment of each *chou*. Thus, the Hsi-shuang Pan-na T'ai autonomous *chou*, established in January 1953, received its seal in June 1953,[39] while the Te-hung T'ai and Ching-p'o autonomous *chou*, established in July 1953, received its seal in January 1954.[40] Kuo Ying-ch'iu, Vice-chairman of the Yunnan People's Government, made the presentations in both instances. Chao Ts'un-hsin, Chairman of the Hsi-shuang Pan-na *chou* People's Government, and Tao Ching-pan, Chairman of the Te-hung *chou* People's Government, were the respective recipients. In his acceptance speech, Chao said that

> Henceforth, people of all nationalities in the Hsi-shuang Pan-na T'ai autonomous area, under the brilliant leadership of the Chinese Communist Party and Chairman Mao and the direct guidance of higher-level people's governments, and with the help of Han people and the Chinese People's Liberation Army who are bravely defending the frontiers of the motherland, must with heart and mind progress further in strengthening the intimate unity of all nationalities and all strata, and in assuring abundant production; and, moreover, increase vigilance so as to immediately prepare to smash the destructive schemes of the American-Chiang bandits in order to protect the blessings already attained by the people of all nationalities and to safeguard the motherland's frontiers.[41]

Tao responded in a similar vein, although the emphasis was now more on economic development (the keynote of the First Five-year Plan), than on defending the frontiers. In presenting the seal, Kuo asserted that

> The establishment of the Te-hung T'ai and Ching-p'o autonomous area is appropriate to this historical period when our country under the leadership of Chairman Mao, the Com-

---

[39] *Yün-nan jih-pao*, July 23, 1953.   [41] *Ibid.*, July 23, 1953.
[40] *Ibid.*, February 24, 1954.

munist Party, and the Central People's Government is progressively actualizing socialist industrialization on a national
scale and steadily realizing the socialist transformation of
agriculture, handicrafts, and private commerce which will
turn this agricultural country of ours into an industrialized
state. . . . The requirement for the autonomous area people's
government is to be a government which will guide opposing
sides in struggle, a government which will guide the people
in unity, and a government which will guide the masses of
each nationality in production; only in this way can the autonomous area government really become the government of
the people of each nationality themselves and effectively exercise the rights of self-government.[42]

This episode of the presentation of seals clearly shows that
the ancient feudal system of the frontier T'ai was still intact
five years after liberation. The Party's desire to curry favor
with the traditional leadership was also reflected in its publicly
enunciated policy of "uniting with the headmen [t'ou-jen],"
as the lower echelon T'ai leaders were called.[43] The hope that
the traditional leadership could be influenced to develop a
"positive attitude" toward the exercise of "home rule" (tang-
chia tso-chu) was the theme of a week-long conference of individual pan-na leaders chaired by Chao Ts'un-hsin which met
at the end of July 1954. He was said to have encouraged chairmen and vice-chairmen of the various pan-na autonomous governments to study the Constitution and to oppose local
nationalist thinking (ti-fang min-tsu chu-i szu-hsiang).[44]

No doubt Tao Ching-pan had similar concerns in mind
when he returned to Mang-shih, administrative center of the
Te-hung chou. If T'ai aristrocracy was in a somewhat less
flourishing condition here than in the Hsi-shuang Pan-na, it
was a fact nevertheless that Chinese Communist political control had still not been firmly established in half the villages
of the chou.[45] Moreover, the strength of Buddhism was such

[42] Ibid., February 24, 1954.   [44] Ibid., September 3, 1954.
[43] Ibid., July 23, 1953.   [45] Jen-min jih-pao, November 4, 1954.

that it was seen by the Party as a major stumbling block to increasing production. Efforts to induce the frontier T'ai farmers to use fertilizer and thereby increase production had been largely frustrated by a reluctance to grow more than what was required for subsistence.[46] One is reminded of the story, told by Wilfred Burchett, of the introduction by the American aid program of chemical fertilizer in Cambodia. When the Buddhist farmers there learned that the yield of their fields would be doubled by the application of fertilizer, they planted only half the acreage that was normally sown.[47]

The six hsien on the western fringe (i.e., the left bank of the Salween) of the Te-hung chou account for most of the chou's T'ai population. "Peaceful, consultative land reform" was supposed to have been completed here at the end of 1955,[48] but little headway in the cooperative movement had been made by the time of the 1957 spring plowing.[49] Moreover, an apathetic attitude on the part of the masses was blamed for serious shortcomings in the land reform movement itself.[50] In the Hsi-shuang Pan-na chou, too, "peaceful, consultative land reform" was said to have been fully implemented by the end of 1955. During the land reform campaign in the Hsi-shuang Pan-na, over five hundred progressive individuals were enlisted into the ranks of the CCP, making it possible to establish Party branches in most of the T'ai villages. Lands belonging to Buddhist temples were not expropriated, yet it was possible to give land to soldiers who had defected from the Kuomintang forces in north Burma.[51] It was later revealed that this land reform involved, in the first instance, dividing up the holdings of the Hsi-shuang Pan-na "king" (hsüan-wei-ssu), and assigning them to the lesser princes (chao-meng); then, with the cooperation of most of the patriotic nobility (ai-kuo shang-ts'eng jen-shih), the farmers came into actual possession of the land they tilled, thus ending an 800-year-old feudal land sys-

[46] Yün-nan jih-pao, February 23, 1957 and October 19, 1957.
[47] Mekong Upstream (Hanoi, 1957), p. 26.
[48] Yün-nan jih-pao, January 12, 1957.
[49] Chung-kuo hsin-wen (news service), April 3, 1957.
[50] Yün-nan jih-pao, October 19, 1957.
[51] Jen-min jih-pao, January 14, 1957.

tem. This process extended into 1956. A uniform land reform movement was carried out among all the frontier T'ai, including those in the Meng-lien T'ai, Lahu, and K'awa autonomous *hsien* and the Keng-ma T'ai and K'awa autonomous *hsien*, both of which lie between the two *chou* I have been discussing. As a result of this land reform, it was said that the typical T'ai farmer received lands producing from 460 to 1200 *chin* (one *chin* is equal to half a kilogram) of grain, and that production suffered no deterioration as a result of land reform.[52]

Land reform was not extended to the hilly areas within these several frontier autonomous areas. The societies of the Ching-p'o, Hani, K'awa, and other peoples living in these uplands, it was said, were not differentiated along class lines. For the time being the Party confined itself to attempts to reform their agriculture so as to eliminate the slash-and-burn (*tao-keng huo-chung*) technique which was characteristic of these hill farmers; it also sought to improve relations between the uplanders and the lowland T'ai. Meanwhile, of course, the PLA was carrying out its work of securing the frontier, special concern being focused on the hills. The Army also undertook extensive land reclamation projects, which must have been located chiefly in the margin between the irrigated fields of the T'ai and the uplands inhabited by the hill peoples.[53] It was no doubt to such new lands that the influx of Han Chinese agriculturalists (including returned overseas Chinese as well as peasants from the interior and deactivated soldiers) was primarily directed. These Han Chinese communities gave the state a reliable base in frontier areas in which there were no pre-existing Han Chinese settlements.

An example of improved relations between uplander and lowlander took place in Ching-p'ing *hsiang* of Lung-chou *hsien* in the Te-hung *chou*. In this township a struggle over water rights had been going on between the Ching-p'o hill farmers and the T'ai paddy cultivators for fifteen years prior to liberation. Relations were so bad that the Ching-p'o did not

[52] *Min-tsu t'uan-chieh*, 1959, No. 7.

[53] In an analogous situation in north Thailand, this author has visited pioneer villages carved out of marginal lands by Kuomintang forces.

descend the mountain on which they lived, nor did the T'ai
ascend it. But after liberation the problem was resolved, allow-
ing the normal economic interdependence between hill and
plain to assert itself once more.[54] A similar improvement in
relations was reported to have occurred between the Hsi-
shuang Pan-na T'ai and the Aini, the *chou*'s most numerous
hill people (30,000 as compared with 120,000 for the T'ai).[55]
The Aini people provide most of the labor for the Hsi-shuang
pan-na's famous tea industry, yet the T'ai viewed them con-
descendingly, as is suggested by the report that the Aini put on
native dances on the occasion of the *chou*'s first anniversary
celebrations, held at Ch'e-li on January 23, 1954.[56] On the
other hand, there were instances of T'ai inviting Aini to come
down off the mountains to take up irrigated agriculture.[57] The
T'ai in the Te-hung *chou* were also said to have made room
in the plains for Ching-p'o families.[58] The relationship between the lowland T'ai and the fire-field K'awa in the two
multinational *hsien* of Keng-ma and Meng-lien seems to have
been a great deal more remote than was the relationship between the T'ai and Ching-p'o in the Te-hung *chou* or that
between the T'ai and Aini in the Hsi-shuang Pan-na; this
alienation was blamed as much on British as on Chinese imperialism in the area.[59] The task of reforming the headhunting
K'awa, ninety percent of whom practiced slash-and-burn agriculture, was left to the PLA.[60]

An accomplishment of great significance for the future of
the Hsi-shuang Pan-na was the opening in December 1954 of
a new highway linking the *chou* capital of Ching-hung (Ch'e-
li) with Kunming, a distance of 741 kilometers.[61] What had
been a month's walk now took only three to five days by bus.

[54] *Yün-nan jih-pao*, August 30, 1957.

[55] *Jen-min jih-pao*, May 21, 1955.

[56] *Yün-nan jih-pao*, January 27, 1954.

[57] *Jen-min jih-pao*, September 29, 1953.

[58] *Kuei-chou jih-pao*, July 24, 1957.

[59] *Chung-kuo hsin-wen* (news service), September 18, 1960.

[60] *Jen-min jih-pao*, September 28, 1958.

[61] *Ibid.*, May 21, 1955, and *Chung-kuo hsin-wen* (news service), August
28, 1956.

It was reported that the new road aroused the patriotic ardor of the T'ai people, although in the old days they had used the expression, "The Han are coming!" to frighten children.[62] The road continued south from Ching-hung to Ta-lo on the Burma border, and therefore became known as the Kun-lo (*Kun*-ming to Ta-*lo*) highway. It was but the most newsworthy part of a new road complex tying the frontier regions to the interior.[63]

In 1957 the T'ai of Yunnan felt the impact of the nation-wide anti-rightist campaign, the issues of which were aired in August at the Fourth Session of the First People's Congress of Yunnan; speeches of the more prominent delegates were carried in the provincial daily.[64] As noted earlier in connection with the provincial Nationalities Institute, this campaign sought to extirpate the influence of the Yunnanese old guard, the leader of which was said to be former governor Lung Yün. It was said that members of the old guard in Yunnan, together with their accomplices who had fled to Hong Kong, were scheming to establish Lung Yün as the "Emperor of Yunnan" (*Yün-nan t'u huang-ti*). Using the slogan of "Yunnan for the Yunnanese" (*T'ien jen ch'ih t'ien*), this clique was reportedly opposing socialism; the non-Han among them were accused of "local nationalist thinking" (*ti-fang min-tsu chu-i szu-hsiang*), reflected in sentiments such as "there being no class contradictions in national minority areas, democratic reform is an invention of the Communist Party"; "land reform is a Han Chinese contrivance"; and "the nationalities did not unite as a result of democratic reform." Participation by Han cadres in frontier land reform was defended by the Party on the grounds that it was essential for the progress of the national minorities and could be opposed only by those who wished to preserve feudalism. Anti-Party activities were especially serious in the Hung-ho Hani and Yi autonomous *chou*, where "illegal land-

[62] *Jen-min jih-pao*, February 29, 1955.

[63] For Yunnan as a whole, the new regime claimed that from 1950 to mid-1957 it had built four times the mileage of roads as had been built during the previous thirty years—that is, since motor roads began to be built in 1921. *Yün-nan jih-pao*, August 25, 1957.

[64] *Yün-nan jih-pao*, August 25, 1957.

lordism" (*pu-fan ti-chu*) had made its appearance and where counter-revolutionaries threatened reprisals if the Party tried to discipline them.

The speech of Chao Tsun-hsin, Chairman of the Hsi-shuang Pan-na *chou* People's Government, was one of those given prominence in the *Yunnan Daily*.[65] He told the assembled delegates of the Yunnan People's Congress that local nationalists in the *chou* continued to oppose the presence of Han cadres. In their view, the realization of regional autonomy obviated the need for CCP leadership and, therefore, of Han cadres, but Chao declared that they were still essential. What the rightists did not seem to understand was that the struggle between the two roads of capitalism and socialism would be a long and difficult one. As long as it continued, Chao said, Han cadres, and especially higher-echelon Party cadres, would be needed. The rightists, for their part, criticized regional autonomy as being artificial. According to Chao, they charged that the *chou* and *hsien* chairmen in the Hsi-shuang Pan-na had responsibilities but no rights and that the national minorities in the *chou* did not enjoy equality (with the Han Chinese). As for the so-called autonomous *chou*, they said, there was not even democracy at the *hsien* level. Such views were characterized by Chao as bourgeois at best. There could be no peace for socialism, he said, nor any end to nationalities oppression, so long as capitalism continued to exist.

Another speaker from the Hsi-shuang pan-na, Vice-chairman Tao Yu-shih, conceded that there had been a great deal of Han participation in the *chou*'s land reform movement, but denied the contention of the rightists that there had been no class contradictions in the Hsi-shuang pan-na and that land reform had alienated, rather than unified, Han and non-Han.[66]

The complaints of the rightists must have been real, for it was just at this time—that is, in 1957—that the exodus of Yunnan T'ai into the Shan State of Burma, the Muong Sing area of Laos, and northern Thailand reached sizeable proportions. This is the testimony, as related to the author, of a leading

[65] *Ibid.*   [66] *Ibid.*

T'ai from the Hsi-shuang Pan-na, who left Yunnan in 1948 but remained in close touch with developments there.[67] As the state took the place of the landlord, agricultural taxation actually increased, and the easy-going T'ai of the Hsi-shuang Pan-na had to work harder than they ever had before.[68] Because of their peace-loving nature, my informant said, they did not offer active resistance to the Han Chinese who flooded into the Hsi-shuang Pan-na, becoming a majority within a dozen years or so. The anti-rightist campaign was the first clear sign of things to come, and it was recognition of this fact that triggered the T'ai exodus.

In retrospect, it can be seen that the united-front tactics employed by the CCP among the T'ai of Yunnan during the early years of the PRC was merely a transitional device, which could be terminated as soon as the Han Chinese apparatus of control was strong enough to risk a more direct form of administration, and that the anti-rightist campaign was the signal for this change. As the PRC became more confident of its ability to control the Hsi-shuang Pan-na, the practice of Buddhism and use of the T'ai language were restricted. However, the soft tactics of the united front were held in readiness for use whenever serious resistance might force the Party to make a tactical retreat.

Evidence of a similar Chinese Communist impact on the Te-hung *chou* was provided by its erstwhile Chairman, Tao Ching-pan, who fled to Burma in late 1957 or early 1958, where he was interviewed by a correspondent of a Rangoon Chinese newspaper.[69] Tao Ching-pan said he had been forced to flee for his life from the oppression of the Chinese Communists. He was accompanied by nine other princely individuals (*t'u-ssu*), all of whom had been accused of "reactionary

[67] This interview, conducted in Chinese, took place on February 1, 1967.

[68] The easy-going life of the good old days was disappearing in northern Thailand, too, where the introduction of tractor technology and a national market system induced the farmers to work harder. See Michael Moerman, *Agricultural Change and Peasant Choice in a Thai Village* (Berkeley and Los Angeles, 1968), especially p. 168.

[69] *Ya-chou jih-pao*, April 1, 1958.

activities" (*fan-tung huo-tung*). He claimed that the promises made to them by the CCP in connection with the establishment of the Te-hung *chou* were now being broken, and that it had become more and more difficult to cooperate. The CCP's national minority policy was very different on the inside, he declared, from what it appeared to be on the outside. He charged specifically that T'ai young men were being drafted and sent to the frontier, and that his people were threatened with extinction. Perhaps the most extraordinary part of Tao Ching-pan's adventures is that somehow the Chinese Communists lured him back to Yunnan, for he reappears at the First Session of the Second Yunnan People's Congress, held in November 1958. On this occasion he not only voiced approval of the socialization of the Yunnan frontier but repeated the verses of a new song from the Te-hung *chou*:

> Our ancestors have labored for thousands of years,
> Each attaining but a small bit of land,
> But now working just a few hundred days,
> We surpass all the long efforts of our ancestors.

Apart from more abundant harvests, he noted that infectious diseases, including malaria, had been effectively checked in the *chou*. The article observed, in concluding, that little more than a month previously Tao had attended a conference in Kunming on establishing guidelines for frontier socialism.[70] It seems likely that, as a price for his return, he won some concessions from the Party. That significant concessions were, on different occasions, made by the Party in favor of the T'ai (Shan) of the Te-hung *chou* was confirmed by a Burmese Shan (T'ai) informant interviewed by the author.[71]

SOCIALIZATION

Late in 1957 the issues in the Party's campaign against local nationalism were summarized in a carefully prepared statement, signed by leading non-Han personalities in the Party

[70] *Ta-kung-pao* (Peking), November 14, 1958.
[71] Conversation with Vichai Kuatrakal (the name used in Thailand by this Shan) of January 12, 1967 in north Thailand.

and government, which appeared in the provincial daily. Entitled "Criticize local nationalism, clearly distinguish the great truths from the great falsehoods in the national minority question" (*P'i-p'an ti-fang min-tsu chu-i, ming-pien min-tsu wen-t'i shang ti ta shih ta fei*),[72] this formulation of the problem made clear the ideological shift to the left which had taken place in the CCP's national minority policy during the preceding eighteen months. As was observed at the beginning of this chapter, the Party line during 1956 had been that socialization of the frontier regions of Yunnan must be tailored to the special characteristics of the non-Han peoples there. The Party now felt that overemphasis of these special characteristics could indefinitely delay the establishment of cooperatives, the main ingredient of socialization. This shift was not peculiar to Yunnan, but was, rather, a nationwide change in direction.

The article pointed out that "national characteristics" (*min-tsu t'e-tien*) had been used by bourgeois nationalists to deny the class struggle and resist socialism. Attributed to them were sayings such as, "Cooperatives are all right for the Han people but are not suitable for the national minorities" and, "There have never been beggars among our national minorities, and without going into cooperatives we can continue to produce in the same way and get along quite well." But the Party countered this line of reasoning by declaring that unless the national minorities joined with the Han Chinese in building cooperatives, the former would be left behind in the transition to socialism, creating intolerable disequilibria within the country. The local nationalists were also criticized for equating Party leadership with Han leadership and for demanding the establishment of separate, national Communist parties as opposed to the unique CCP. But the Party insisted that "regional autonomy" was not just an empty formula and that Party cadres among the national minorities were not simply "running dogs of the Han Chinese" (*Han-tsu tsou-kou*). To explain large-scale Han participation in transforming the "backward face" of the frontier, the Party resorted to its ultimate justification for its whole approach to the national mi-

[72] *Yün-nan jih-pao*, December 29, 1957.

nority question: namely, that imperialist aggression in China had inextricably bound together all the people of the country.

Concluding their case against the local nationalists, the authors of the article declared that the issue at hand was nothing less than a struggle between two types of perspectives and policies concerning nationalities—that of the proletariat and that of the capitalists. This situation, it was averred, reflected the low ideological level of many national minority cadres, explicable in terms of the brief duration of the democratic reform movement and the rapidity of cadre training. Moreover, most of the national minority cadres did not even come from the un-propertied class (*wu-chan chieh-chi*), so it was inevitable that they would take a long time to fully imbibe Marxism-Leninism. The situation was serious; local nationalism even reached into the top echelons of CCP cadres among the national minorities.[73] At stake was the very question of whether the national minorities and the Han people would be able to make the transition to socialism together. As a corrective measure, the training of nationality cadres needed to be greatly improved, while the older cadres needed to remake themselves (*kai-tso tzu-chi*); at the same time, the problem of great-Han chauvinism could not be ignored, it was said.

This intensification of the campaign against local nationalism had been immediately preceded by a "frontier work conference" (*pien-chiang kung-tso hui-i*) of the Yunnan CCP committee, which set the "basic direction" for the cooperative movement on the frontier. The conference, which met in Kunming from December 10 to 20, 1957, affirmed that all nationalities must travel the socialist road together. While admitting that there were real differences among the various nationalities, the Party insisted that the argument of "special characteristics" absolutely could not be used to deflect a national minority from the socialist path. The commitment to this path was firm (*chien-te*), and cooperatives were an essential ingredient of it. The Party claimed that the first batch of agricultural cooperatives, introduced on the frontier during the past year, had been well received by the people. The two thousand and more

[73] *Ibid.*

cooperatives thus far established accounted for twenty-two percent of those peasant households (mainly among those classified as "poor peasant" and "lower-middle peasant" families) which had completed land reform; they had realized production increases of ten to twenty percent, with most in the range of fifteen to twenty percent. As a result, the people's livelihood had been improved and nationalities unity enhanced.[74]

In light of the Party's determination to proceed with the cooperative movement among the frontier nationalities, as revealed in the decisions of the December meeting, it can be seen that the attack on local nationalists was meant to neutralize non-Han opponents of the cooperatives. The initial justification for the establishment of cooperatives among the wet-rice farmers of the Te-hung, Hsi-shuang Pan-na, and Hung-ho *chou* had been that, having destroyed feudalism by means of the land reform movement, the peasants now had to pool their resources in order to rationalize production. Land reform was but a stage on the road to socialism.[75] Thus, there was to be but a brief period of nominal private ownership of land to serve as a link between feudalism and socialism. The alternative to cooperativization was the development of capitalism: this is what was meant by the phrase, "struggle between two roads" (of capitalism and socialism), frequently used in the literature of the period[76] to describe the post-land-reform situation in the countryside.

Inasmuch as Yunnan's frontier feudalism had involved a complex pattern of rights and duties, as opposed to privileges of ownership,[77] the cooperative movement was but an intensification of a campaign to overturn a whole way of life. Small wonder that it encountered opposition right from the beginning. But it had its supporters as well. Thus, we are told that the T'ai farmers in a frontier village of Jui-li *hsien*, in the Te-hung *chou*, were converted to the cooperative movement in the course of a local "socialist education" (*she-hui chu-i chiao-*

[74] *Chung-kuo hsin-wen* (news service), December 26, 1957.

[75] *Kuang-ming jih-pao*, February 8, 1957.

[76] For instance, *Yün-nan jih-pao*, October 19, 1957.

[77] The categories of feudal tenure among Yunnan's T'ai people were delineated in *Kuang-ming jih-pao*, March 1, 1957.

yü) program. One of them is reported to have said that, "After these several days of discussion, I can now see that following the old way is not good—for that is the way of exploitation and oppression. Cooperatives are good—that is the way without exploitation and oppression, where everybody works and everybody has food and clothing."[78]

A complementary situation prevailed among the hill peoples on the frontier who, in the categorization of Marxist historiography, had not yet entered the feudal stage of social evolution. Despite the lack of class antagonism among these uplanders, cooperatives were being organized among them at the same time that the cooperative movement was being pushed among the lowlanders.[79] This is what was meant by "leaping over" one or several stages of "social development" referred to by, among others, Professor Lin Yueh-hua of Academia Sinica.[80] The T'ai, for example, would have leaped over one stage—capitalism—whereas the hill peoples would have leaped over two stages—feudalism and capitalism—on their road to socialism. This interpretation was presented in the provincial daily under the caption, "Transcend one or several stages of social evolution; the national minorities of our province pass over to socialism; regions with more than seventy percent of the national minority population of the whole province have been cooperativized."[81] During 1957, five hundred agricultural producer cooperatives, embracing ten thousand households, were said to have been established among the Lisu, Ching-p'o, K'awa, and other frontier uplanders. A prominent feature of this effort was improving the agricultural technique of the hill peoples; it was reported that fifty thousand mou of land had been opened up and a thousand aqueducts constructed. Many farmers who formerly practiced

[78] *Yün-nan jih-pao*, November 1, 1957.

[79] *Kuang-ming jih-pao*, March 2, 1957.

[80] "The Minority Peoples of Yunnan," *China Reconstructs*, 10, 12 (December 1961).

[81] "*Ch'ao-yüeh i-ko huo ji-ko she-hui fa-chan chieh-tuan; wo-shen shao-shu min-tsu k'ua-ju she-hui chu-i, chan ch'üan-shen shao-shu min-tsu jen-k'ou 70% i-shang ti ti-ch'ü i ho-tso-hua*," *Yün-nan jih-pao*, September 28, 1957.

slash-and-burn agriculture now farmed irrigated fields,[82] the study of Han and T'ai methods being an important part of this transition. In the Ching-p'o areas of the Te-hung *chou* alone, seventeen hill stations for the diffusion of advanced agricultural technique were established during the spring of 1956.[83]

The cooperativization of rural society on the Yunnan frontier stretched into 1958, overlapping with the country's next major mass movement, the Great Leap Forward, and merged almost imperceptibly with the commune movement of 1959. The process of socialization, which started late on the frontier as compared with the interior, was therefore telescoped, with both uplanders and lowlanders experiencing the waves of different mass campaigns in rapid succession. An outstanding feature of this process seems to have been the Party's determination to stimulate greater production through greater regimentation. With each successive wave, the peculiar features of the national minorities were more and more discounted by the Party and Government apparatus charged with policy implementation, and the content of regional autonomy was correspondingly diminished.

The Great Leap Forward was heralded by a mass campaign to build irrigation works and expand agricultural production launched in the winter of 1957–58. The campaign was featured prominently in the *Yunnan Daily* of December 19, 1957. The paper noted in an editorial that of the province's forty-one million *mou* of farm land, only fifteen million were in watered fields ([*shui*] *t'ien*), whereas the remaining twenty-five million *mou*, or sixty-one percent of the total, were in open, unwatered fields ([*han*] *ti*). (One *mou* is equal to one-sixth of an acre.) In some areas, such as Li-chiang special district in the north, the proportion of watered to dry fields dropped to one in four. Most of Yunnan's rain falls in the summer and autumn, the editorial observed, with little precipitation in winter and spring. In many areas, even drinking water for man and his farm animals became extremely scarce during the dry season. Water conservation projects, especially in hilly areas, could

[82] *Ta-kung-pao*, January 16, 1958.
[83] *Kuang-ming jih-pao*, March 2, 1957.

therefore have a dramatic effect on the productivity and well-being of a large proportion of Yunnan's rural population. To "regulate the water [so as] to irrigate the land" (*wen-ting shui chiao ti*) had the effect of approximately doubling output. The hill peoples marveled at the newly built aqueducts, which traversed the mountains, bringing water from sources dozens of *li* distant: "The treasure comes gurgling in!" (*hua-hua ti t'ang-lai le yin-tzu*), they exclaimed.[84]

Headlines in the same issue of the *Yunnan Daily* read as follows: "People of all frontier nationalities positively echo the Party's call; correctly respond to the initial great forward surge in the agricultural production high tide" (*Pien-chiang k'o tsu jen-min chi-chi hsiang-ying tang ti hao-chao; cheng hsiang nung-ye sheng-chan kao-ch'ao ti ti-i ko kao feng t'ing-chin*). Surveying the situation in various parts of the province, the paper observed that "positive elements" (*chi-chi fen-tzu*) from agricultural villages in three *hsien* of the Nu-chiang Lisu autonomous *chou* had held a rally to study and discuss the National Agricultural Development Plan (*Ch'üan-kuo nung-ye fa-chan kang-yao*) and that during the winter and spring it was expected that 35,000 *mou* of irrigated fields (*shui-t'ien*) would be opened up in the *chou*.[85] In the Te-hung T'ai and Ching-p'o autonomous *chou* there were plans to build medium and small scale irrigation projects capable of serving 25,000 *mou* of agricultural land. The manpower requirements for the works in the Te-hung *chou* called for the mobilization of more than 40,000 laborers of all nationalities, while in the Hsi-shuang Pan-na T'ai autonomous *chou*, a "great water-works army" (*shui-li ta-chün*) of 50,000 people had been organized. Similar schemes were being unfolded in the Hung-ho Hani and Yi autonomous *chou* and other frontier areas.[86]

Responding to the directives of the second session of the CCP's Eighth National Congress, which formally initiated the Great Leap Forward (*ta t'iao chin*) in socialist production and socialist transformation, the Party committee for Yunnan

[84] *Yün-nan jih-pao*, December 19, 1957.   [86] *Ibid.*
[85] *Ibid.*

province in May 1958 laid down three basic tasks for the frontier nationalities.[87] The first of these "transformations" (kai-pien) concerned the physical basis of frontier agriculture. In mountainous areas, terraced fields were to be constructed to take the place of the fire-fields traditionally used by the semi-nomadic slash-and-burn agriculturalists, while in lowland areas the application of fertilizer was to be promoted. The second transformation was to take place within the societies of the various nationalities, each of which, from their different points of departure, was to develop production relationships appropriate to socialism. The third transformation was to be spiritual and cultural, aimed chiefly at the eradication of superstitious beliefs.

These three transformations had already been in progress for several months and would be continued. The Party maintained that the changes they were effecting in frontier society would astonish bourgeois anthropologists (tzu-chan chieh-chi min-tsu hsüeh-chia), who characterized such peoples as "remnant societies" (ts'an-ts'un she-hui).[88]

The Great Leap Forward was credited with having produced a fifty percent increase in the agricultural output of the Yunnanese frontier in 1958 as compared with 1957. With this firm foundation, local industries had sprung up everywhere. Factory production and mining had also spurted. At the end of 1958, every village and cooperative had its own industry, and an army of several hundred thousand iron and steel workers was laboring night and day. Trade, education, and health had developed, too. Thus, the transformation of the societies of the frontier nationalities was proceeding rapidly, and relationships between the different peoples were being improved. The people's admiration for socialism was said to have increased with their potential for production, and in some places they had begun to form peoples' communes (jen-min kung-she).[89]

Discussing these developments, Chang Chung, Vice-chair-

[87] Kuang-ming jih-pao, June 19, 1958.
[88] Ibid.
[89] Yün-nan jih-pao, November 8, 1958.

man of the Yunnan People's Government, said that they revealed the wisdom of Mao's concept of "uninterrupted revolution" (*pu-tuan ko-ming*) as well as the accuracy of Mao's observation that the condition of poverty and blankness favored revolution (*i ch'iung erh pai, ch'iung tse szu pien*). The frontier being even "blanker" (*keng pai*) than the interior regions of the province, the saying "to want results is to want revolution" (*yao kan, yao ko-ming*) was even more applicable to the masses there. Chang made it clear, however, that Party members still harbored preconceptions about the "backwardness" (*lo-hou*) of the frontier nationalities and that this was an impediment to the fulfillment of the Party's responsibility for facilitating their transformation. Although he thus implied that the masses were ahead of the Party in their revolutionary zeal, he indicated that "the struggle between the two roads [of capitalism and socialism] had still not been completely resolved" (*liang t'iao-lu t'ou-cheng hai wei wan-ch'üan chieh-chüeh*). Whereas the task of "communization" (*kung-she hua*) had been basically completed in the interior of the province, it was still at an incipient stage among the frontier nationalities. A "socialist and communist education movement" (*she-hui chu-i ho kung-chan chu-i chiao-yü yün-tung*) was about to be initiated among the frontier nationalities. Chang let it be known that in the course of the anti-rightist and other campaigns carried out during the past year, the revolutionary ranks had been infiltrated by "bad elements" (*huai fen-tzu*), who fanned the flames of local nationalism. Firmer Party leadership was essential, he concluded.[90]

Cooperativization, still incomplete at the time of the launching of the Great Leap Forward, had been fully realized by early in 1959, and communes had been established in fifty percent of the area in which land reform of the democratic, consultative variety had been carried out. Yet productivity remained too low to permit the Party to be complacent about the prospects for the commune movement, which was its immediate task. That difficulties thus far encountered in the socialization of the frontier had obliged the Party to reassess its

[90] *Ibid.*

methods was made explicit in a *Yunnan Daily* editorial of February 1959. Seeking an answer to the question of how to quickly raise production among the frontier nationalities, the Party turned its attention once again to the recently discredited line of reasoning which emphasized the importance of peculiar national features (*min-tsu t'e-tien*). The national minorities simply had not made the response to the CCP program that had been expected of them. Apparently, the productive force of the people had not really been set free by democratic, consultative land reform, and the cooperatives exhibited economic, ideological, and organizational inadequacies. Thus, the "transformation of the original production relationships" (*kai-pien yüan-lai ti sheng-chan kuan-hsi*), which should already have been completed, remained as a continuing task of the commune movement.[91]

This ideological retrenchment included a reaffirmation of the policy of cooperation with upper-level personages (*shang-ts'eng jen-shih*). It was freely admitted that individuals of the national minorities who had, prior to the establishment of the PRC, claimed feudal titles once recognized by the Chinese imperial bureaucracy, had been accepted by the Chinese Communists as legitimate leaders of their respective nationalities. Thus, *t'u-ssu* (feudal lords), *shu-kuan* (subordinate officials), *shan-kuan* (mountain mandarins), and *wang-tzu* (princes) frequently became chairmen (*chang*) of *chou*, *hsien*, or *ch'ü* people's governments or became delegates to the national or provincial people's congresses. In uniting with (*t'uan chieh*), educating (*chiao-yü*), and transforming (*kai-tsao*) such persons, the Party frequently had them attend one of the Nationalities Institutes or sent them on trips to Peking and on tours around the country. In the land reform movement they received only the same allotment as everyone else, and they formally enjoyed only the same political rights as the rest of the people, but the Party had clearly taken steps to insure that their lives would be tolerably comfortable. As recently as August 1958 the provincial Party committee had brought nearly three hundred such upper-level personages to Kunming for

[91] *Ibid.*, February 27, 1959.

the purpose of familiarizing them with national policy concerning the building of socialism. Some of them had subsequently entered the government bureaucracy, while others
decided to remain with their people in the transition to
socialism.[92]

The benefits for Yunnan's frontier nationalities of socialism
as compared with feudalism were stated quantitatively in the
People's Daily in June 1959. It was claimed that between 1952
and 1958—that is, before and after land reform and the initia-
tion of the cooperative movement—annual per capita output
of food grains among the lowland agriculturalists more than
doubled, from 393 to 657 *chin*, and in the Great Leap Forward
year of 1958 it increased even more rapidly, attaining a level
of 1,000 chin. The superiority of the cooperatives was said to
have been revealed in the fact that productivity among the 22
percent of the peasant households who had joined the 2,707
cooperatives established through the end of the year 1957 had
increased by 20 to 30 percent, whereas the increase had been
only 10 to 15 percent among those families which had not yet
joined. Presumably for this reason, the number of cooperatives
on the frontier jumped to 6,379 in 1958, by which time communes were beginning to appear.[93]

In April 1960 a joint presentation was made to the second
session of the Third National People's Congress by national
minority leaders from the Yunnan frontier. Chao Ts'un-hsin
and Tao Ching-pan were among the twenty-five notables who
signed the document, which was delivered as a single speech.
Entitled, "Guided by the general line [for the building of
socialism], the people of all nationalities on the frontier of
Yunnan leap forward and again leap forward,"[94] this statement lauded the achievements of the frontier nationalities
during ten years of Chinese Communist control. According to

[92] "*T'uan-chieh, chiao-yü, kai-tsao*" (unite, educate, transform), *Jen-
min jih-pao*, September 24, 1959. My informants in north Thailand sometimes referred to this policy as "brainwashing."
[93] "*Pien-chiang jen-min sheng-huo hsin-hsin shang-jung*" (Livelihood
of the frontier peoples revives joyously), *Ibid.*, June 14, 1959.
[94] "*Tsai tsung-lu-hsien ti chih-yin hsia yün-nan pien-chiang k'o tsu
jen-min t'iao-chin tsai t'iao-chin*," *Ibid.*, April 14, 1960.

this document, more than ninety percent of the agriculturalists on the frontier had joined cooperatives, which were established in accordance with the peculiarities of the frontier and the special features of the people there. We are told that the cooperatives spurred production, enhanced the unity of the majority (that is, not all) of the people, and strengthened the defenses of the motherland. The minorities, according to the statement, were catching up to the level of the Han people: whereas it was formerly said, "We are not capable of using the advanced production methods of the Han Chinese [farmers]," it was now said that, "What our Han Chinese elder brothers can manage, we, too, can definitely accomplish." (An example of this fact was that the non-Han farmers of the frontier lowlands now applied human and animal manure to their fields.)

One of the most noteworthy features of the document was the unqualified welcome it extended to Han colonists on behalf of the frontier peoples. The numbers and productive strength of the latter, it pointed out, were insufficient to rapidly develop the rich potential of the frontier, and this was an urgent national task in the building of socialism. In addition to people of the Han and other comparatively advanced nationalities of the interior, youth (from all over the country, and not merely from the Yunnanese interior) and returned overseas Chinese (notably from Indonesia), were specifically mentioned as being needed. According to the document, all such newcomers had received and would continue to receive an enthusiastic welcome from the national minorities on the frontier of Yunnan.[95]

[95] *Ibid.* This influx would account for what my T'ai Lü informant (see above, note 67) described as the virtual assimilation of his people by the Han Chinese in the Hsi-shuang pan-na.

6

ECONOMIC ASPECTS OF REGIONAL AUTONOMY IN KWANGSI

HE doctrine of regional autonomy, the cornerstone of the PRC's national minority policy, is essentially political in nature. It provides formal guarantees to each nationality that it will enjoy a degree of self-government. This self-government, however, does not extend to control over the natural wealth of the autonomous areas. Rather, the whole country is to be developed as a single unit; it is assumed that this development will be as advantageous to the national minorities as to the Han majority. In a sense, then, the PRC's formal policy towards its non-Han peoples may be seen as a means to an end, rather than an end in itself, and this end is not merely the ideological reorientation of the national minorities but also the economic incorporation of their territories.[1]

[1] There would seem to be a parallel between the direction of national minority policy in the PRC and the process of decolonization in the mari-

For many years prior to the establishment of the PRC, China's frontier regions had suffered economic hardships owing to the disorders that had plagued the country. Production and sale of local products and commercial crops (*t'u-chan t'e-chan*) had declined; consequently, daily necessities (*jih-yung pi-shu p'in*) such as table salt and iron cooking pots had become increasingly scarce. At a high-level conference on trade in the frontier regions, it was said that the national minorities in Kwangsi had told the Chinese Communists: "Had you arrived a month later, we would all have starved to death." Accordingly, the conference resolved that an urgent effort must be made to reopen commercial channels with national minority areas. The report on the conference proceedings was made to the State Council by Kuo Li-chuang, Minister of Trade in the CPG (Central People's Government). Kuo noted that 396 local products from national minority regions all over the country had been exhibited at the conference.[2]

In Pai-se special district (later to become the core area of the West Kwangsi Chuang autonomous *chou*), the State Trading Company (*Kuo-ying mao-i kung-ssu*) began operating with two units in April 1951, which was as soon as the security situation would allow. By June 1952, there were fifty-five units, while the number of employees (eighty percent of whom were Chuang) had increased five-fold. The value of local products purchased during 1951 reached 27.9 million *yüan*; manufactured articles sold during the same period were valued at 50.9 million *yüan*; trade in early 1952 was running fifty percent above the 1951 level. Making a special effort to reach the minority peoples in the hills, cadres went out with pack horses, porters, and push carts. Thanks to the exertions of mobile teams operating in the mountains, the terms of trade were altered to the advantage of the minority peoples. One *chin* of

---

time empires of the European powers. In both East and West we may observe an emphasis on economic development in the less advanced, peripheral areas which serve the vital interests of the metropolitan (now, "neo-colonialist") nations, whether European, American, or Han Chinese.

[2] *Yün-nan jih-pao*, December 23, 1951.

tea oil, which previously had been traded for half a *chin* of salt, was now worth more than three *chin* of salt; the exchange value of aniseed had increased two and a half times. Thus, the purchasing power and well-being of the hill people had risen considerably.[3]

Another instance of improved living conditions resulting from Chinese Communist trade policies was reported from a Yao village in Wu-suan *hsien* northwest of Nanning. In this mountain village of six hundred persons, salt and other daily necessities had been very scarce owing to the village's poor communications, but with the establishment there of a branch of the Wu-suan Trading Company early in 1952, it was no longer possible for private merchants to exploit the Yao people.[4] On the other hand, the Communist trading firm for San-chiang *hsien* (later, the San-chiang T'ung autonomous *hsien*) was criticized for bringing in strange items such as socks, towels, and toothbrushes, for which there was no demand, instead of essential goods like cotton yarn, rice, salt, and farm tools.[5]

Attractive trade opportunities were meant to supplement patriotic appeals as an inducement to the minority peoples to increase output. Moreover, as laid down by a conference called by the Kwangsi province ccp Committee in November 1951, production was to take precedence over class struggle in national minority areas. "It is essential," the conference had resolved, "to unite all strata [*chieh-ts'eng*] in the effort to increase production."[6] The same conference took note of various shortcomings in trade work thus far, including an irresponsible attitude on the part of many cadres. There had not been enough leadership, enforcement, or investigation. As a result, the funds dispersed by the State Trading Company in the form of relief, loans, and investments, had not had the desired effect. In some cases, loans actually made by the state were not

[3] *Kuang-hsi jih-pao*, June 5, 1952. A new note issue of 1955 replaced the inflated *yüan* of the early PRC years. For a discussion of PRC currency, see Audrey Donnithorne, *China's Economic System* (London, 1967), pp. 414 ff.

[4] *Kuang-hsi jih-pao*, May 25, 1952.   [6] *Ibid.*, June 24, 1952.

[5] *Ibid.*, June 4, 1952.

getting into the hands of the farmers, indicating the existence of corruption.[7]

By the beginning of 1953 the Nationalities Affairs Commission for Kwangsi province was able to declare that, thanks to the efforts of the State Trading Company, outlets for the important local and special products had been opened up for the minority peoples of Kwangsi. As a result, price ratios had been improved for the local people and production had been substantially increased. There had been a fifty percent increase in the number of commercial units (*mao-i chi-kou*) in the West Kwangsi Chuang autonomous area between 1952 and 1953, while the number of such units for the national minority regions of the whole province had risen to 371. A special effort had been made in the outlying mountain regions, such as the Lung-lin multinational autonomous area. Thus, whereas in Ling-lo *hsien* private merchants had paid only 31,250 *yüan* for one *tan* (equals 50 kilograms) of aniseed, the price paid by the State Trading Company was 252,000 *yüan*, seven times higher; in Ning-ming *hsien*, the price for forest mulberry had doubled. In Pai-se the value of (locally produced) rice in relation to salt had increased fifty percent. Improved terms of trade for the national minorities was made possible by better transportation facilities: 900 kilometers of highways had been built during the previous few years, and practicable waterways had been extended by 500 kilometers. An increase in the price of lard (locally produced from pig fat) from 300 to 600 *yüan* per *chin* in Ta-hsin *hsien* was directly attributable to a new road.[8]

An example of the results achieved by the vigorous trade policy of the new regime was the delivery of tea oil and tung oil (a wood product) from Feng-shan *hsien* in the West Kwangsi Chuang autonomous area. Before 1949, these local products could not be sold due to the lack of communications. With the establishment of the Feng-shan branch of the State Trading Company, however, things began to change. Using pack horses brought in from Yunnan, the trade cadres succeeded in delivering 146 tons of tea oil and tung oil to the state during the

[7] *Ibid.*   [8] *Ibid.*, February 9, 1954.

twelve-month period ending in April 1954. In return, more than 50,000 *chin* of industrial products such as kerosene and cotton cloth were taken into Feng-shan. This success was said to have derived in part from greater attention being paid to local tastes, and to better opportunities being made available to local people within the trading organization.[9] Another reason for the success of Feng-shan in boosting production was the installation, early in 1954, of its first mechanical oil-pressing plant. Most of the Chuang and Yao farmers of the *hsien* grow tea trees on the hillsides. In the whole *hsien*, the trees cover an area of 25,000 *mou*, making it Kwangsi's leading producer of tea oil. Tea oil (*ch'a yu*) is pressed from the *Camelia sasanqua* and is valued both as a food product and as an industrial raw material. The new oil-pressing plant, which represented a large investment on the part of the provincial People's Government, was able to process 2,000 to 2,500 *chin* of camelia seeds per day.[10]

The Wu-p'ai River valley which traverses several *hsien* in northern Kwangsi possesses outstanding timber resources which the PRC began exploiting at the end of 1952. The Miao, Yao, and other hill peoples who live in this area had been unable to derive any economic advantage from the beautiful firs (*shan-shu, ts'ung-shu*) in this area due to the difficulty of negotiating the river. But then the forestry bureau of Kwangsi province sent personnel to study the situation and dredging operations began late in 1953. A series of rapids which the "Kuomintang reactionaries" had unsuccessfully blasted on three separate occasions were overcome by the Communist labor brigades in twenty-five days. The workers braved the icy waters despite bitter winter weather (in this mountainous area the temperature frequently drops below zero) and, with the help of a crane to remove large boulders, were able to complete their task.[11]

At the beginning of the work, officials from the forestry bureau announced to the hill peoples in the Wu-p'ai area that,

[9] *Ibid.*, June 5, 1954.   [11] *Ibid.*, April 2, 1954.
[10] *Ibid.*, April 9, 1954.

> The timber in this area of yours is very great in quantity and of excellent quality. Soon the State will send men to open up the river so as to get at your timber. At that time your lives will become much better.

The people were overjoyed by this news, we are told, but many did not believe that the People's Government would be able to clear the rapids. The evident sympathy among some people here for the Nationalists derived, apparently, from the fact that the latter had operated in villages near the Hunan-Kwangsi border, traversed by the Wu-p'ai River, for a comparatively long period of time. The river was quickly opened up, however, and the people enthusiastically began selling their timber to the State. This was of great importance, for "with the industrialization of the country, the demand for timber was increasing daily." After being sent down the Wu-p'ai to Liu-chow, south China's leading wood-processing center, trees from this region in northern Kwangsi are turned into a variety of products which are sent to such faraway places as Sinkiang and Inner Mongolia. A typical response to the changes brought by the opening up of the Wu-p'ai River was that of the hill tribesman who was quoted as saying:

> The advantages of industrialization are vast; our land of "ox-horned peaks" [niu-chiao chien] has experienced an amazing transformation during the past few years, with our lives every day becoming sweeter and sweeter.[12]

THE TA-YAO-SHAN

The area of the Ta-yao-shan produces a wide variety of medicinal and edible plants, indigo and other dye-producing plants, tung and tea seeds, and other natural products which had a long-established market in Canton and Hongkong.[13] As soon as they arrived on the scene, the Chinese Communists exhorted the people here to improve the quality and increase the output of their local products.[14] Early in 1952 the People's

12 Ibid.
13 Ibid., June 12, 1952.
14 Ibid., December 22, 1951.

Government made available large-scale financial assistance to the people of the Ta-yao-shan in the expectation that it would help them restore and expand forestry production. (Funds from all sources—CPG, Central-south Region, provincial—amounted to 2.2 million *yüan*.) This intention was made explicit in meetings held in each *hsiang* at the time the relief was distributed, and the people were assisted with seed, tools, and draft animals so as to immediately bring about an enlargement of the area planted under such commercial crops as tea trees and tung trees.[15] At the same time, trading facilities were being set up to link the area with the rest of the country.[16] Mobile teams trekked to each village to carry out "propaganda, investigations, and trade work."

During July (1952), agreements were made for the purchase of more than forty products from the Ta-yao-shan, the contracts reaching a value of over 60 million *yüan*. The principal products covered by these agreements were tung seeds and tung oil, tea seeds and tea oil, water lily grain (*i-mi*), peanuts, uncured tobacco, tea leaves, lily flour (*pai-ho fen*), miscellaneous flours, dried bamboo shoots, hemp, cinnamon, mushrooms, and bamboo paper. Handicraft producers among the Yao people were also said to have been aided in increasing production.[17]

In the spring of the following year a campaign was launched to increase the productivity of the tea industry in the Ta-yao-shan. As a result of this "tea-planting movement" (*chih-ch'a yün-tung*), 56,000 *chin* of tea seeds were planted in the spring of 1953 as compared with 23,000 *chin* in the spring of 1952. The campaign of 1953 was necessitated, it seems, by the fact that a large part of the tea planted the previous year did not produce shoots.[18]

Emphasis on tea remained strong in 1954, as the notion of "turning Ta-yao-shan into one beautiful tea garden" took hold in Party and Government circles. From 1951 to 1954, we are told, 87,000 *chin* of tea seeds were brought into the Ta-yao-shan from elsewhere (including Hunan province as well as

[15] *Ibid.*, July 16 and July 30, 1952.
[16] *Ibid.*, October 4, 1952.
[17] *Ibid.*, September 10, 1952.
[18] *Ibid.*, April 2, 1953.

other *hsien* within Kwangsi). During the same period, heavy expenditures were made for tools and equipment and many outside cadres were brought in to supervise the planting of seeds, preparation of the ground, and transplanting. During April 1954, meetings were held in seven districts of Ta-yao-shan autonomous *hsien* to discuss problems of tea production. Emphasis was placed on improving the quality of the tea; it was noted that the higher the grade of tea leaf, the higher the price. Part of Ta-yao-shan's tea crop was earmarked by the China National Tea Company (*chung-kuo ch'a-yeh kung-ssu*) for shipment to the people's democracies of the Soviet bloc.[19]

A report of 1955 observed that among items produced in the Ta-yao-shan area, there were important industrial raw materials and medicinal herbs as well as foods. No less than fifty different products were of commercial significance. Thus, the Ta-yao-shan's importance to the industrialization of the country was readily appreciated. According to the same report, the resources of the area were little known or exploited before 1949, but all of this had changed with "the postive opening up of the Ta-yao-shan by the Communist Party and the People's Government for purposes of trade." This "opening up" began in May 1952, at the same time regional autonomy was being implemented in the Ta-yao-shan. Output of tung and tea seeds, to take two outstanding examples of local products from the Ta-yao-shan, had increased rapidly. Total tung seed production in 1953 was 933 *tan*, compared to 3,236 *tan* for the *first five months* of 1954; tea seed production during the same period had jumped from 89 to 857 *tan*. Interestingly, no exception was made for producers of commercial crops in connection with the Party's program of socialization; thus, in 1954, cooperatives were being formed among the Ta-yao-shan's forestry workers. One way in which the Yao people were said to have been rewarded for the increased rate of exploitation of the Ta-yao-shan was in greatly expanded health and education facilities.[20]

[19] *Ibid.*, June 9, 1954.
[20] *Nan-fang jih-pao*, January 15, 1955.

MOUNTAIN COOPERATIVES

It took only a few years of experience in working with the upland minorities of Kwangsi to convince the Party of the necessity of tailoring its policies to meet the special features of these societies. This was the burden of an enlarged meeting of the CCP's Pai-se Committee which held a three-day conference in late October 1955 to consider the resolutions of the recently convened plenum of the Seventh CCP Congress concerning the cooperative movement. Although these resolutions made it clear that cooperatives would have to be established in mountainous as well as lowland areas, considerable latitude remained as to the specific ways in which cooperatives could be adapted to hill conditions. With proper guidance, the meeting concluded, the cooperative movement among the upland minorities could definitely be a success, bringing about an increase in the production of industrial raw materials. That there was some doubt on this point, however, was indicated by the widespread "rightist" notion that the peculiarities (*t'e-shu*) of the hill peoples would obstruct the cooperative movement.[21]

The problem for the Han Chinese was how to supervise cooperativization among peoples whose way of life was alien to their own. Paddy fields (*shui-t'ien*) were totally absent in many national minority areas of Kwangsi. In addition to commercial crops, many of these uplanders raised livestock, so that animal herding was one of the specific types of economic enterprise with which the CCP had to deal in the cooperative movement. In the Tu-an Yao autonomous *hsien*, for instance, there were 110,000 goats in the fall of 1956, and the local authorities had immediate plans for raising the size of the herds to 150,000 head. Medicinal herbs and other local products were also important, and the trade bureau was busy developing them. Of Tu-an's 325 "agricultural" cooperatives (*nung-yeh she*), 159 were counted as "mountain cooperatives" (*shan-she*) and 68 as "hill cooperatives" (*pan-shan she*), leaving a maximum of 98 for cooperatives primarily engaged in wet-rice agriculture.

[21] *Kuang-hsi jih-pao*, November 8, 1955.

Presumably, the Yao of the mountain cooperatives were slash-and-burn agriculturalists, if not primarily herders or herb-collectors. The task of a three-level (*hsien*, district, village) cadre conference held in Tu-an from September 23 to October 4, 1956, was to "investigate all aspects of expanding production of the mountain areas" (*yen-chiu ch'üan-mien fa-chan shan-ch'ü sheng-ch'an*).[22]

In a mountain village of P'ing-kuo (formerly P'ing-chih) *hsien* in Pai-se special district (West Kwangsi Chuang autonomous area) a cooperative was formed in the fall of 1954 to bring together into one economic unit Chuang agriculturalists and Yao herders.[23] This approach was widely used in Kwangsi during the socialist "high tide" of 1955/56. "Joint cooperatives" (*lien-ho she*) was the term applied to cooperatives which knit together two or more nationalities and their respective economic pursuits. The idea of the joint cooperative was—apart from promoting "nationalities unity"—to take advantage of the strong points (*t'e-chang*) of each nationality, and, in particular, to put to good use the energies of the Yao, Miao, and T'ung mountaineers who, it was noted, were frequently slash-and-burn agriculturalists. Some joint cooperatives were criticized because the divisions of labor within them did not sufficiently reflect nationality characteristics.[24]

A joint cooperative in the Hsi-shan (West Mountain) district of the Pa-ma Yao autonomous *hsien* embraced people of the Han, Chuang, and Yao nationalities. Instead of all going out together to work at the same tasks, the Yao members of the cooperative spent most of their time working in the dry, upland fields, while the Chuang and Han members worked mainly in the irrigated fields. The division of labor along national lines was also reflected, it was claimed, in the secondary industries (*fu-yeh*) of the cooperative: Yao members wove bamboo hats, which were then varnished by Chuang members. Han members were made responsible for the care of the coopera-

[22] *Ibid.*, October 14, 1956.   [24] *Ibid.*, April 19, 1956.
[23] *Ibid.*, December 9, 1954.

tive's pigs, and care of the cattle and sheep was assigned to Chuang and Yao members.[25]

In the Ta-yao-shan, we are told, the "mutual-aid and cooperative-production movement" was carried out in accordance with the "special features of mountain regions" (*shan-ch'ü t'e-tien*) so as to heighten nationalities unity, patriotism, and enthusiasm for socialism. Concurrently, there were big advances in trade, education, and health work.[26]

In another predominantly Yao area, Tung-shan *hsien* in southeastern Kwangsi, 99.9 percent of the farming households were said to have been cooperativized by the spring of 1956. In this *hsien*, the Han people were established in the valley bottoms, where they practiced wet-rice agriculture, while the Yao practiced fire-field agriculture in the hills. Although not described as "joint cooperatives," the cooperatives in Tung-shan *hsien* were said to have promoted harmony between the Yao and Han and to have made possible a gradual breaking down of the differences which, historically, had kept them apart. Han-Yao cooperation was said to have helped make it possible to increase production of both grain and local products. That the special features of the area were taken into account in Tung-shan's cooperative movement is apparent in the term "mountain socialism" (*shan-ch'ü she-hui chu-i*) applied to the transformation reportedly taking place there.[27] Despite the Ta-yao-shan CCP Committee's efforts to wed the cooperative movement to the ecology of the uplanders, however, there were many mistakes and inadequacies, as was made clear at the *hsien*'s Second People's Congress. Although the productivity of the upland minorities had been increased at the same time cooperativization was carried through to completion (99.3 percent), many delegates criticized various government organs (*cheng-fu k'o pu-men*) for ineptness. In particular, the unique

[25] *Ibid.*, September 7, 1956. According to *Kuang-hsi jih-pao*, April 30, 1957, a number of Yao families from the Hsi-shan district had been relocated in a Chuang village of Pa-ma *hsien* in 1952, but we are not told the reason for this move.

[26] *Kuang-ming jih-pao*, May 25, 1956.

[27] *Kuang-hsi jih-pao*, September 7, 1956.

features of the production methods employed by the non-Han Chinese had not been sufficiently heeded; consequently, there had been definite mistakes in the attempted improvement of those methods.[28]

The situation of the Yao in relation to the cooperative movement was evidently even worse in other places. The Yao of I-chou village, I-shan *hsien,* had refused to join with the Han and Chuang in the cooperative movement out of fear that their customs would be trampled upon. Among the "Indigo" Yao of T'ien-lin *hsien,* killing an ox was a sacrificial act, performed so as to appease the spirits, but they were no longer able to do this after their oxen had been cooperativized. "Without spirit worship, we are just like the Han," they said. Such cultural phenomena could not be regarded lightly, it was declared, for they were reflections of basic livelihood patterns.[29]

The cooperatives also came under fire at a meeting convened by the Pai-se special district CCP Committee in late August 1956. Among the 185 representatives of the Yao, Miao, Chuang, and other minority peoples of the district, many voiced the opinion that leadership of the cooperative movement among the hill peoples had shown insufficient regard for the special characteristics of the local people. It was charged that in some areas the indigo fields tended by Yao women and hemp fields tended by Miao women had been incorporated into the cooperatives without prior consultation. It was not unusual for individual (Han) cadres to curse the "evil and tyrannous customs" (*ya-pa tso-feng*) of the uplanders. Sometimes failure to observe local practices adversely affected production, as in Lung-lin multinational autonomous *hsien,* where a field which usually yielded 1,300 *chin* of rice had yielded only 900 *chin* in 1956. The reason for this set-back was the attempt by outsiders to realize two crops rather than the traditional single crop: because of the short growing season, the second crop had not matured.[30]

[28] *Ibid.,* January 18, 1957.   [30] *Ibid.,* September 5, 1956.
[29] *Ibid.,* February 23, 1957.

To overcome such shortcomings, the Pai-se Committee in mid-September dispatched investigation teams to examine more thoroughly the local conditions (*ti-ch'ü t'e-tien*) prevailing in different parts of its area of jurisdiction. On the basis of these findings, a meeting of responsible officials and cadres met in late November and deliberated for nearly a month. The result was a "production plan" (*sheng-ch'an kuei-hua*) for 1957 which was based on the specific conditions prevailing in lowland (*p'ing-yüan*), hilly (*t'u-shan*), and mountainous (*shih-shan*) regions. Whereas in 1956 the patterns of production in lowland areas had often been taken as the standard for judging production in upland areas, the 1957 plan provided for markedly different emphasis according to terrain. Grain production would be emphasized in lowland and some hilly areas, but it should not be pushed in upland areas, which could more advantageously be used for forestry or animal husbandry. The earlier investigation had revealed that of the Pai-se area's 1,593 villages, 232 were in lowlands, 506 in infertile mountains, and 855 in hilly regions.[31]

It is interesting to note that there is no explicit reference to cooperatives in the above-mentioned work plan for Pai-se, although the corrective measures in the plan seem to answer criticisms of the cooperatives then being heard. This suggests that the State's overriding concern with production was independent of the cooperative movement; put another way, the cooperatives should serve the purposes of expanding production, but production should not be sacrificed for the purposes of the cooperatives. In Yunnan, similarly, the requirement to increase production in hilly areas completely overshadowed the establishment of autonomous areas.

The cooperative movement also had little relevance for the local paper industry in Ta-miao-shan, for even prior to the advent of the cooperative movement, this 500-year-old craft had been virtually destroyed by the Communists themselves. By their own admission, the output of this local industry, which had averaged 14,500 *tan* per year before 1949, had dwindled steadily: one village that had produced 800 *tan* in

[31] *Ibid.*, January 1, 1957.

1952 had ceased production altogether by 1956; in three other villages, output had fallen forty percent between 1952 and 1956. The regional market which this paper had always enjoyed was threatened by factory-made paper, which became more readily available under the PRC. In what must be regarded as a classic instance of Han-chauvinist thinking, Party cadres did not appreciate the value of the local product, which was accordingly priced so low that many of the Miao villagers who had been part of the paper industry began cutting and selling the particular species of bamboo (nan-chu) from which the paper was made. By 1956, as a result of these cumulative effects, many experienced paper-makers found themselves working as farm laborers in agricultural cooperatives. Of 398 persons in Szu-yung district who had formerly been in the paper industry, only 29, in one tiny paper-producing cooperative, still made paper; the remaining 369 had joined agricultural cooperatives.[32]

In this specific instance, at least, the PRC's policy of regional autonomy for national minorities had conspicuously failed to safeguard the well-being of the people. Indeed, the nationwide industrialization plans of the PRC seem to have been in conflict with its national minority policy, and the latter was the loser. The cooperative movement does not appear to have had any effect one way or the other: it merely institutionalized an unhappy situation.

CHANGING AGRICULTURAL TECHNIQUES

The gulf between the ecology of the T'ung uplanders and the Han-Chuang lowlanders may be suggested by the fact that tigers had always been an ever-present hazard in the area of the San-chiang T'ung autonomous hsien, nestled in the mountains of the Kweichow-Hunan-Kwangsi frontier. When the Communists arrived they found that tigers, in addition to killing livestock, were in some places preventing the T'ung farmers from cultivating their fields at higher elevations. A "hunting movement" (ta-lieh yün-tung) launched in the spring of 1953 netted fourteen tigers, four leopards, fifty-one

[32] Ibid., June 23, 1956.

wild boars, forty-nine foxes, and one gore (*shan-niu*), not to mention over 500 antelope (*shan-yang*).[33]

The traditional agricultural technology among the T'ung was relatively primitive. Though they used the plow, it was pulled by man rather than beast; the embankments around the fields were made with a hoe; and the fields were weeded by hand. Consequently, productivity was very low. Enthused by the Great Leap Forward, the Party took drastic measures to change this state of affairs. One of its slogans was that "Every *mou* should produce a thousand *chin* of grain"; some "rightists" countered with the charge that "The Great Leap Forward can produce a thousand *chin* of troubles." By eliminating many traditional festival days, the Party boasted of having greatly increased the number of working days in the year. It also introduced double-cropping on a large scale. Of the 150,000 *mou* of paddy fields in the entire *hsien*, most produced only one crop, and glutinous rice (*lo-mi*) was the standard grain. In 1958, however, 100,000 *mou* were scheduled for double-cropping; deep plowing had become standard and modern tools were in general use. The introduction of carts and wooden boats had brought about a revolution in transportation; mountainous areas were now reached by air transport lines. Tents had been provided so as to enable the farmers to live closer to the fields they tilled, and water-storage basins had been dug on the average of one for every ten *mou* of irrigated fields. On the basis of this "leap forward" in agriculture, local industries had also expanded: by the middle of June 1958 there were more than 1,100 newly established processing plants and mining facilities in operation.[34]

These reforms were carried out amidst quite a bitter struggle between the ccp and "local nationalists." Owing to the "complex situation" (*fu-tsa ch'ing-k'uang*) prevailing in the area—a reference, probably, to the prolonged activities of kmt "bandits"—and to the fact that "peaceful land reform" (*ho-p'ing t'u-kai*) had been implemented there, the pre-existing

[33] *Ibid.*, May 13, 1953.   [34] *Ibid.*, July 17, 1958.

class structure had been left pretty much intact right down to the inauguration of the Great Leap Forward. The cooperative movement, begun shakily in 1955 on the basis of peasant households classified as "poor" (*p'in-nung*) and "middle" (*chung-nung*), was threatened in 1957 by the withdrawal of peasants from the cooperatives that had been established. Declaring that the cooperatives had been forced upon them by Han cadres, the local "rightists" maintained that among the people of San-chiang it was "nationality contradictions" (*min-tsu mao-tun*) which were critical, while class differences (*chieh-chi ch'ü-pieh*) were comparatively unimportant. The Party, however, called for a "rectification campaign" (*cheng-feng*) among the whole people in order to refurbish the tarnished image of socialism.[35]

Slash-and-burn agriculture (*tao-keng huo-chung*) was a special target of the reform efforts of the Party in the field of agriculture. Before liberation, this method of farming was in general use throughout most of the upland area of Pai-se special district, including the Lung-lin multinational autonomous *hsien*. In 1953, the government moved isolated groups of families from mountain regions to low-lying areas, but comparatively few of the hill people were affected. Beginning in 1955, the Party tried to make use of the cooperative movement in its campaign to transform the farming practices of the uplanders. The introduction of double-cropping reportedly led to substantial increases in output per *mou*. In Lung-lin *hsien* for 1956 it was planned to sow 13,000 *mou* to early-ripening maize and 40,000 *mou* to a first crop of rice. For the whole of Pai-se special district, the increase in the acreage sown to a first crop in 1956 was three to four times greater than that for 1955.[36] The key to the agricultural transformation desired by the Party were the irrigation works that were being vigorously promoted throughout the district: for the West Kwangsi Chuang autonomous *chou* (of which Pai-se is a part), 74,000 big, medium, and small scale water conservation projects, capable of

[35] *Kuang-ming jih-pao*, October 30, 1958.
[36] *Kuang-hsi jih-pao*, February 10, 1956.

irrigating several million *mou* of paddy fields, had been carried out by the beginning of 1956.[37]

According to the Party, Chuang agricultural techniques also needed "transformation." The Han farmer was a harder working, more efficient producer than the Chuang farmer. Perhaps because of this, the typical Han farmer in Pai-se *hsien* cultivated half again as much land as the average Chuang farmer. And while the Chuang grew little besides rice, depending on wild vegetables and pumpkins to supplement his diet, the Han always kept a vegetable garden and usually grew a secondary crop such as sugar cane. The standard of living of the Han household was correspondingly higher than that of the Chuang household.[38]

Like the T'ai in Yunnan, the Chuang in Kwangsi did not systematically apply human and animal manure (*jen, ch'u fenniao*) to their fields, as did the Han Chinese. Education campaigns were launched as early as 1953 to induce the Chuang people to build privies so as to collect their excreta for later application to the fields. Sties were built so as to facilitate the collection of pig manure.

At a meeting of Kwangsi "model workers" (*lao-tung mu-fan tai-piao*) from the national minorities held in early 1958, the establishment of privies in most of the cooperatives in non-Han regions of the province was held to be one of the outstanding accomplishments of the revolution in Kwangsi, making it possible to apply an average of 40 to 60 *tan* of manure per *mou* of cultivated land throughout the province.[39] Systematic manuring made possible the continuous use of all their fields, whereas in the past the Chuang had been obliged to fallow their lands. Another element of the Han people's advanced agricultural technology which they brought to the Chuang was the transplanting of rice seedlings from special seed beds, rather than broadcasting the seed directly on the fields, as the Chuang had always done. The new regime was able to demonstrate that by such means productivity per *mou* could be dou-

---

[37] *Ibid.*, July 31, 1957.
[38] *Ibid.*, December 4, 1952.

[39] *Ibid.*, March 8, 1958.

bled.[40] Having increased by some fifty percent the food production of the national minority areas of Kwangsi, the Party could claim by 1956 that these areas had become self-sufficient in food and therefore no longer required shipments from Han areas to make up their food deficit. A large proportion of the grain produced annually was thereby released for other purposes having to do with the Party's goal of the economic transformation of the whole country.[41]

URBANIZATION

To conclude this chapter, it remains to comment briefly on the growth of towns and cities as an index of the changes brought about in Kwangsi by the new regime. In particular, Nanning, the capital of the Kwangsi Chuang Autonomous Region, and Pai-se, which lies closer to the heartland of the Chuang people, will be discussed. The growth of industry in Kwangsi, put at over 1000 percent between 1950 and 1958,[42] is reflected in the process of urbanization.

Nanning and Pai-se are linked by a navigable river, the Yu-chiang, which was dredged in 1954. A motor road, which follows the Yu-chiang, was extended from Pai-se into Yunnan in 1955. Also in 1955, a rail link was opened between Nanning and North Vietnam.[43] From Nanning, rail and river transport lines reach neighboring provinces as well as other major towns of Kwangsi.

Although Nanning was the nominal capital of the West Kwangsi Chuang autonomous area (chou) from its inception in 1952, Pai-se was its real nerve center.[44] With a population of about 20,000, Pai-se had by 1956 become a production center rather than simply a consumption center. Whereas it had previously had one or two companies engaged in rice milling and tobacco processing, it now produced agricultural imple-

[40] Ibid., March 25 and May 26, 1953.

[41] Ibid., July 31, 1957.

[42] Kuang-hsi chuang-tsu tzu-chih-ch'ü (The Kwangsi Chuang Autonomous Region), (Peking, 1958).

[43] Ta-kung-pao (Hong Kong), June 27, 1955.

[44] Chung-kuo hsin-wen (news service), July 23, 1956. The autonomous area was redesignated a chou in March 1956.

ments, paper, and soap, and had printing, dyeing and weaving, and oil-pressing plants, as well as water and electric utilities. The industries at Pai-se served as a processing and manufacturing center for the rural population spread along the Yu-chiang River in thirteen *hsien* within Kwangsi as well as in eastern Yunnan and southern Kweichow. For example, the Pai-se Special District People's Factory had turned out 150,000 pieces of agricultural equipment from its establishment in 1951 until April 1956. Among these tools were water pumps, threshing machines, and plows, and they were credited with having made possible the eradication of slash-and-burn practices and the attainment of an abundant food supply. This same factory underwent an expansion during early 1956 that gave it an annual capacity of 60,000 to 80,000 modern plows or other implements. In the same year, additional power generating facilities were under construction to meet Pai-se's expanding industrial demand.[45]

By 1962, the port of Pai-se was handling over 100,000 tons of cargo per year; the steamer downstream to Nanning took only a day and a half to cover the 410 kilometers between the two cities. A road network radiating from Pai-se linked all fifteen *hsien* of the special district, each of which had daily bus service to and from the city. There was also regular bus service to Nanning, Kunming, and Kweiyang (capital of Kweichow province). In Pai-se itself, the streets were lined with schools, cinemas, and public buildings, and the passersby were largely Chuang, Yao, Miao, and other nationalities in their native dress. This modern city stood in sharp contrast to the Pai-se of pre-liberation days, a remote town famous only for its opium dens and brothels.[46]

Nanning, too, had a completely new aspect. In terms of area, by 1956 Nanning had grown from a pre-liberation town of 4.5 square kilometers to a city of 86.5 square kilometers; if the newly acquired empty space adjacent to the city were included, to 128 square kilometers. During the same period of time, the area covered by buildings had nearly tripled, from 270,000 to

[45] *Ibid.*   [46] *Ibid.*, October 26, 1962.

775,000 square meters. Both the number of workers in industry and the number of households engaged in handicrafts increased five times between 1950 and 1956. There were also four new hospitals and four new institutions of higher education, plus ten new institutions at the middle-school level. In 1951 a people's park was built on the old KMT execution grounds, where many revolutionary warriors had met their end, and a library was added in 1953.[47]

Between 1950 and 1959 Nanning's population jumped from 80,000 to 560,000. During the same period the number of industrial establishments and business enterprises had increased from a bare handful to 600, and these were capable of producing 1,300 different kinds of machine-made goods. Culturally, Nanning now had nine theaters, which, in addition to showing the latest motion pictures, featured Chuang drama as well as Peking and Canton opera. To allow ample room for future growth and to give it administrative control over nearby agricultural lands, the area under the city's jurisdiction was increased to 2,300 square kilometers.[48]

A new industrial sector, which sprang up on reclaimed land on the west side of the city, included, in addition to a railway station, an electric generating plant, machine shops, brick and tile works, smelting and refining, chemicals, and meat packing. On the south side of the city, across the Yung River, were located iron and steel, sugar, and paper plants. North of the city there were new parks and recreational facilities.[49] Whereas Nanning had previously been a center for consuming imported goods, symbolized by Coca-Cola (*k'o-k'ou-k'o-lo*), it now produced most of the consumer goods required by the city and the surrounding countryside.[50]

[47] *Jen-min jih-pao*, March 23, 1956.
[48] *Chung-kuo hsin-wen* (news service), June 1, 1959.
[49] *Ibid.*, November 7, 1959.   [50] *Ibid.*, November 20, 1962.

7
TRANS-FRONTIER
RELATIONS

THE transformation of the southern frontier of China wrought by the PRC has fundamentally altered the Middle Kingdom's relations with its neighbors in Southeast Asia. This transformation is an aspect of the overall strengthening of China in relation to the outside powers whose empires formerly extended to the south China frontier region. As foreign influence receded, the pre-existing pattern of relationships between "elder brother" China and her "younger brother" neighbors began to reassert itself.[1] Despite the fact that (as of early 1970) this process has been increasingly challenged by the United States, the south China frontier is still stronger, relative to the power of adjacent states, than it has been at any time in the past—at least since the Taiping rebellion. Implementation of the CCP's policy of national regional autonomy among the minority peoples of Yunnan and Kwangsi has facilitated both the integration of these two provinces into the developmental process being carried forward elsewhere in the

[1] Chou En-lai spoke in precisely these terms in an airport speech at Phnom Penh in November 1956, heard by the present author.

country and the establishment of the central government's authority in the border regions.

The relevance of minority policy to frontier security is dramatized by the different situations prevailing among China's neighbors to the south. With the exception of North Vietnam (the Democratic Republic of Vietnam, or DRV), none of these states has carried out effective policies to deal with their minorities. In Laos, government inattention to the problems of the hill peoples has fueled the Pathet Lao movement and led to the virtual detachment of at least two borders provinces—Sam Neua by the DRV and Phong Saly by the PRC—and to the alienation of all the upland areas of the country. The Lao government today is the effective government only of the population strung along the Mekong River and its tributaries; any influence over the hill peoples is exerted by the United States.[2]

In Thailand, similarly, it is the United States which seeks to contain fissiparous tendencies among the hill peoples. So great is the Thai government's indifference to the uplanders, nevertheless, that its authority has been steadily eroded in the mountains along the northern sector of the Thai-Lao border, to the advantage of the Pathet Lao movement.[3]

Although Nationalist forces still provide some stability in northwestern Thailand, their exodus from north Burma coincided with the outbreak of the Shan-Burman war in 1959/60. Military action by the Shans was prompted by steadily mounting oppression of the Shan people by the Burmese army, the increasing ethno-centrism of the Burmese government, and the inability of the Shans to gain redress under the federal constitution of 1948.[4] Whether or not their grievances are exploited

[2] These observations on the Laotian situation are based on current news reports as well as personal visits to that country.

[3] First-hand observations on the situation in Thailand have been supplemented by the author's participation in a seminar on "Counter-Insurgency in Thailand" held at the National War College, Washington, D. C., March 11, 1970.

[4] Personal communication of May 8, 1967, from an officer of the Shan State Army.

by Communists (internal or external), the unhappy situation of the minority peoples in Burma, Thailand, and Laos is a serious liability to the governments of those states. Politically, the hill peoples of Assam are similarly situated. Taken together, the plight of these minority peoples, located on one of the front lines of the "cold war" in Asia, raises the specter of a broad struggle between Communist and anti-Communist forces in the proximity of China's southern frontier.[5]

Attention in this chapter will be focused on the role of the non-Han Chinese in Yunnan and Kwangsi in China's relations with Burma and North Vietnam. Down to 1965, the two outstanding features of the trans-frontier relations between the DRV and Kwangsi were, first of all, the national minority policy of the DRV itself, and, secondly, participation by North Vietnamese minorities in the establishment of the Kwangsi Chuang Autonomous Region. The anti-US war effort has dominated Kwangsi-DRV relations in the past half decade. There is only incidental involvement of the national minorities in the trans-frontier relations between the DRV and Yunnan, which pertain mainly to the Hanoi-Kunming railroad.[6] However, the minorities of Yunnan, like those of Kwangsi, have been called on to support the DRV in its contest with the United States. With respect to the trans-frontier relations between Yunnan and Burma, the national minorities were involved in the settlement of the disputed frontier and in the subsequent visit to Yunnan of Prime Minister U Nu, but since 1962 Yunnan-Burma relations have deteriorated.

In this chapter, Laos, Thailand, and Assam will be ignored, not because the PRC does not have a vital interest in these states but because the trans-frontier relations in these three cases do not bear directly upon the evolution of the non-Han peoples in south China, except to the extent that the PRC's national

[5] See Robert Dickson Crane, "Asia's Next War?" in *The Observer*, June 23, 1968.

[6] A 177-kilometer section of this railroad, from the border at Ho-k'ou northward to Pi-se-chai, near Meng-tzu, was torn up by the Nationalists in 1942 to discourage Japanese penetration of Yunnan. Service was not restored until fifteen years later, at the end of 1957. *Yün-nan jih-pao*, December 19, 1957.

minority policy has sought, in general, to appeal to neighboring peoples. It ought to be noted, however, that the presence in Laos of Chinese Communist military construction troops, engaged in road-building and protected by anti-aircraft batteries, has been acknowledged by Prime Minister Souvanna Phouma[7] and that Defense Minister Lin Piao has publicly asserted the PRC's backing of the Pathet Lao movement.[8] It is worth remarking, too, that Peking has long harbored a Thai government in exile under former Prime Minister Pridi Phanomyong and that on February 5, 1965, it openly called for the overthrow of the Bangkok government.[9] Finally, it must be noted that the Naga guerrillas in Assam have reportedly received some training in China and that Chinese arms have been captured by Indian forces fighting them.[10]

MINORITY POLICY IN THE DRV

The provisions of the 1960 Constitution of the Democratic Republic of Vietnam regarding the status of national minorities are virtually identical with those of the PRC Constitution. They provide for equality and autonomy within a unified, multinational state.[11] Prior to the promulgation of the 1960 Constitution, a decree concerning the establishment of autonomous areas in the DRV had been issued on April 29, 1955. On May 7, 1955, there came into being the Thai-Meo Autonomous Region, the name of which was subsequently changed to Tay Bac (Northwest) Autonomous Region. The Tay Bac AR embraces an area equivalent to three provinces in the mountains between the Red River valley and the Laotian

[7] The New York Times, December 15, 1969.

[8] Ibid., January 20, 1970.

[9] New York Herald Tribune (Paris edition), August 4, 1965; The Observer, August 22, 1965.

[10] The Times, June 10, 1968.

[11] Viet Chung, "National Minorities and Nationality Policy in the DRV," in Nguyen Khak Vien (ed.), Mountain Regions and National Minorities in the DR of Vietnam, Vietnamese Studies, No. 15 (Hanoi, 1968). Interestingly, the DRV Constitution of 1946 does not contain such provisions: see Bernard B. Fall, The Viet-Minh Regime, Southeast Asia Program, Data Paper No. 14 (Cornell University and the Institute of Pacific Relations, 1954).

frontier. On the north, it borders on Yunnan province. Its area of over 36,000 square kilometers is one-fifth that of the entire area of the DRV; its population of 500,000 includes 25 different nationalities, the most important of which are the Thai (T'ai) and Meo (Miao).

The Viet Bac (North) Autonomous Region, established on August 19, 1956, is of about the same size as the Tay Bac AR but its population of 1.5 million is three times larger. The Viet Bac AR is located in the uplands between the Red River valley and Kwangsi. It incorporates six provinces and fourteen different nationalities, the largest of which are the Tay (Tho) and Nung.[12] These two autonomous regions, the only two thus far established in the DRV, extend along most of the border with China, and the dominant ethnic groups here are closely related to those in Yunnan and Kwangsi.

As in China, the main thrust of nationalities policy in the DRV is the social and economic transformation of the minority peoples. Malaria eradication, the building and staffing of schools and hospitals, increased production of commercial crops, electrification, and modernization of transport and communication facilities have been some of the immediate targets of the Vietnamese Workers' (Communist) Party in the national minority areas. As in Kwangsi and Yunnan, a special effort has been made to bring into closer harmony the predominantly upland economy of the minorities with the wet-rice agriculture and modern industries of the lowlanders. Irrigation works have been constructed in the hills so as to make possible double-cropping. At the urging of the state, nearly a million Viet (Kinh) lowlanders have settled in the uplands of the Tay Bac AR and Viet Bac AR to help the minorities develop their natural resources.[13]

In an article translated from the Vietnamese which appeared in the Chinese theoretical journal, *Nationalities Research,*[14]

[12] Nguyen Khak Vien, *op. cit.*
[13] *Ibid.*
[14] Lü Wen Lu (this is the Chinese [Mandarin] rendering of his Vietnamese name), "Yüeh-nan shao-shu min-tsu kai-k'uaug" (A general view of the national minorities of Vietnam), *Min-tsu yen-chiu,* No. 7 (Peking, 1959), pp. 28–36.

it was made clear that the rationale for the national minority policy of the DRV was, as in the PRC, anti-imperialism. Since Vietnam had been a colony, all the national groups of the country, the Viet majority as well as the minorities, had been oppressed by imperialism. With the August revolution of 1945, it was claimed, all the peoples of Vietnam joined together in throwing off Japanese and French colonial rule. Indeed, the upland regions inhabited by the non-Viet people were among the principal battlegrounds of the anti-colonial struggle. In particular, the area of the present-day Viet Bac AR is considered to have been the cradle of the Vietnamese revolution. The area of the Tay Bac AR, in which Dien Bien Phu is located, is also considered to have been of great strategic significance. It is claimed that the minorities gladly joined with the Viet people in the anti-French struggle, and that all are bound together in opposition to American imperialism.

With the attainment of military victory in the northern half of the country, according to the same article, the Viet and the minority peoples have been working together to wipe out all vestiges of the colonial and semi-feudal past. Mutual-aid teams and agricultural producers' cooperatives have been organized in the uplands as well as in the lowlands. Per-capita production of maize, an upland crop, was three times greater in 1957 than it had been in 1939, and the purchasing power of the minority peoples in the corn-growing areas had increased four times. Output of forestry products doubled in 1957 as compared with 1956, while the growth of handicrafts had by 1958 enabled the uplanders to produce a significant proportion of their farm tools and daily necessities. These same developments had helped in the campaign to eliminate slash-and-burn agriculture. It was admitted, however, that a great deal remained to be done in relation to the persistent differences in standards of living between the upland and lowland peoples and the continuing existence of great-nation chauvinism and local nationalism.[15]

Writing in the Peking *People's Daily* on the occasion of the fifteenth anniversary of the founding of the DRV, the Chairman

[15] *Ibid.*

of the Viet Bac AR remarked upon the close friendship and cooperation which existed between the minority peoples on each side of the frontier. He noted that minorities such as the Chuang, Miao, and Yao actually straddled the frontier, and that those on one side always came to the aid of those on the other in times of need. For example, the people on the Vietnamese side of the border helped in the suppression of us-Chiang Kai-shek (*mei-chiang*) supporters hidden on the frontier, while the people on the Chinese side of the border actively assisted Vietnam's anti-French struggle. Thanks to their propinquity to Kwangsi and the socialization taking place there, the building of cooperatives and people's communes had been more rapid among the minorities living adjacent to the frontier than it had been among those elsewhere in the Viet Bac AR.[16]

THE VIET BAC A. R. DELEGATION TO THE FOUNDING OF THE KWANGSI CHUANG A. R.

Of the not infrequent visits back and forth between the minorities of south China and the minorities of the DRV, the most important seems to have been that occasioned by the establishment of the Kwangsi Chuang Autonomous Region in 1958. Before describing that event, however, it must be mentioned that a delegation from Kwangsi had witnessed the establishment of the Viet Bac AR in 1956. The thirteen-man delegation from Kwangsi had included individuals of the Chuang, Yao, Miao, T'ung, and Han nationalities, led by the Chuang chairman of the West Kwangsi Chuang autonomous *chou*. Crossing the frontier on August 7, the delegates were said to have been amazed at the similarities between the speech and customs of the people here and those in their native Kwangsi. In addition to attending the celebrations marking the establishment of the Viet Bac AR, the delegation traveled

[16] Chu Wen Chin (Mandarin rendering), "Yüeh-chung pien-chieh k'o tsu jen-min hsi-shou shang she-hui chu-i mai-chin" (People of all nationalities on the Sino-Vietnamese border go forward hand in hand toward socialism), *Jen-min jih-pao*, September 2, 1960.

to Hanoi and elsewhere in the DRV, being enthusiastically received wherever they went.[17]

The Viet Bac AR delegation's attendance at the meeting which formally established the Kwangsi Chuang AR was prominently featured in the national press. We are told that the delegation arrived in Nanning on a special train at 11:15 on March 3, 1958, and that they were welcomed at the station by more than 4,000 workers, cadres, students, and other citizens of the city. The visiting party of twenty persons was led by Chu Wen Chin (Mandarin rendering), Chairman of the Viet Bac AR government and member of the Vietnam Workers' Party. Various nationalities were represented among the delegates, several of whom were women. The most prominent individual among the welcomers was Wei Kuo-ch'ing (a Chuang), Chairman of the Preparatory Committee for the Kwangsi Chuang Autonomous Region. Wei and Chu embraced each other when they met at the station, while youths came forward to present flowers to the delegates.[18]

Wei recalled in his welcoming speech that Kwangsi had sent a delegation to the inauguration of the Viet Bac AR a year and a half previously. That visit, he declared, together with the current one, were two happy landmarks in the friendship of the Chinese and Vietnamese peoples. "Although we are divided between two countries," he said, "the establishment of the Viet Bac Autonomous Region and the Kwangsi Chuang Autonomous Region are, in the same way [t'ung-yang], glorious victories for the nationalities policy of Marxism-Leninism." In his reply, Chu noted that because they adjoined one

[17] T'ai Chen-wu (the T'ung Vice-chairman of the Nationalities Affairs Commission for Kwangsi province), "Chung-yüeh liang-kuo k'o min-tsu ti hsiung-ti yu-i—chi wo-kuo kuang-hsi shen min-tsu tai-piao t'uan-ti yüeh-nan chih hsing" (The fraternal friendship of the various nationalities of China and Vietnam—commemorating the visit of the nationality delegation from our country's Kwangsi province to Vietnam), *Kuang-hsi jih-pao*, October 26, 1956.

[18] *Jen-min jih-pao*, March 4, 1958. A version of the same story (both citing a New China News Agency wire from Nanning dated March 3) which appeared in *Kuang-ming jih-pao* of March 4, says that the two leaders merely shook hands.

another, relations between Kwangsi and the Viet Bac AR were of special significance for Sino-Vietnamese friendship. Elaborating on this theme, he observed that the peoples of Kwangsi and Viet Bac were united by historical as well as geographical ties, and that they shared many cultural traits.[19]

Chu spoke in the same vein later when he addressed the inaugural session of the People's Congress of the Kwangsi Chuang Autonomous Region. Endorsing the PRC's nationalities policy, he remarked that China and Vietnam had the same enemies: imperialism and feudalism. He added (rather pathetically in light of more recent developments), that during the three years since the restoration of peace in the DRV the economy of his country had been restored and advances made in the march toward socialism.[20]

Another noteworthy visit to China on the part of national minorities from the DRV was made in 1959, on the occasion of the PRC's tenth anniversary. A delegation from the Thai-Meo (Tay Bac) AR journeyed to Kunming for the festivities, arriving there on September 28 and departing from Kunming on October 17. While in Yunnan the visitors inspected factories, people's communes, and the Nationalities Institute in Kunming. On their way home, they stopped over at the Hung-ho Hani and Yi autonomous *chou*.[21]

KWANGSI AND THE VIETNAM WAR

Due to the increasingly tense situation along China's southern frontier in recent years, policy with respect to the national minorities there has become explicitly subservient to the security interests of the Chinese state as a whole. In February 1965, rallies were held throughout the Kwangsi frontier region to denounce American aggression. The 38,000 persons who gathered in the eleven *hsien* seats along the Vietnamese border included Chuang, Yao, and Miao, as well as Han.[22] In the early summer of the same year, rallies of non-Han people were held

[19] *Ibid.*
[20] *Jen-min jih-pao*, March 6, 1958.
[21] *Ibid.*, September 30 and October 18, 1959.
[22] *Ibid.*, February 2, 1965.

in both Kunming and Nanning to demonstrate against US aggression in Vietnam.[23]

Kwangsi also found itself directly engaged with "US imperialism" in the coastal area, formerly a part of Kwangtung, which had just come under the province's jurisdiction. In October 1965, Kwangsi fishermen of the Tung-hsing multinational autonomous *hsien* and the town of Hai-pei, both situated on the Gulf of Tongking, gathered to denounce the American bombing of one of their boats west of Hainan Island. One fisherman was said to have been injured. Reportedly, Chinese fishing boats had been attacked on other occasions as well. The demonstrators called on the PLA Air Force units stationed in Kwangsi to prevent further occurrences of such "criminal acts" by the United States.[24] Alleged intrusions by US aircraft over Kwangsi were even more common than incidents on the high seas; Yunnan also complained of having had its air space violated.[25]

A commander of the military sub-district of Nanning declared in June 1965 that

> U.S. imperialism is now conducting more new military adventures in Southeast Asia, ordering its troops to take a direct part in combat in South Vietnam. This shows that US imperialism is heading towards a Korean-style aggressive war. Our Nanning District adjoins the DRV. With US imperialism expanding its aggressive war in Vietnam, we must launch a new upsurge of the study of Chairman Mao's works, strengthen the revolutionization of the units, and make definite preparations in every way for combat, to be ready at any time to support the Vietnamese people in their just, patriotic struggle against America.[26]

A similar line was propounded the following year by a secretary of the CCP Committee for the Kwangsi AR, but by this

---

[23] *Min-tsu t'uan-chieh*, May–June 1965.

[24] *Chung-kuo hsin-wen* (news service), Canton, October 8, 1965.

[25] For instance, Peking Radio on May 12 and 13, 1966 reported the intrusion of five US planes over Yunnan and charged that they had shot down a Chinese plane on a training mission. BBC Monitoring Service, *Summary of World Broadcasts*, Part III, No. 2161.

[26] *Ibid.*, III-1899, Nanning broadcast of June 20, 1965.

time, as the Cultural Revolution gathered momentum, a closer association was made between the thought of Mao Tse-tung and national security:

Kwangsi is on the front line of national defense. Onerous war preparations are also upon our shoulders. All people with awareness in our country understand a truth from their personal experience—that is, whether it is fighting against domestic and foreign class enemies or against nature in production and construction, the most powerful and decisive weapon is Mao Tse-tung's thinking. . . .

The Secretary was speaking to a meeting of two thousand Maoist activists, many of whom were non-Han persons.[27]

The Tu-an Yao autonomous *hsien* was among those parts of Kwangsi mentioned in 1966 as areas in which Red Guards were actively attacking "old ideology, culture, customs, and habits."[28] However, Wei Kuo-ch'ing, First Secretary of the Kwangsi CCP Committee, made it clear that the Mao-study campaign was to be carried out among the masses in all parts of the Autonomous Region.[29] Nanning radio reported in October 1966, for example, that a "mobilization meeting" to advance the Mao-study campaign had been held in the city under the auspices of the Kwangsi Military District.[30]

NATIONALITIES FRIENDSHIP ON THE SINO-BURMESE BORDER

In December 1956 a great meeting dedicated to the furtherance of friendship between the minority peoples of Yunnan and Burma was held at Mang-shih (Lü-hsi), in the Te-hung T'ai and Ching-p'o autonomous *chou*. Mang-shih, situated on the Burma road, is only a few kilometers from the border-crossing point of Wan-t'ing, where agreement on the Five Principles of Peaceful Coexistence had been reached between the two countries in 1954. A Westerner who visited Mang-shih in 1962 said it was similar to towns in northern Burma, except

[27] *Ibid.*, III-2106, Nanning broadcast of February 24, 1966.
[28] *Ibid.*, III-2258, Nanning broadcast of September 4, 1966.
[29] *Ibid.*, III-2217, Nanning broadcast of July 7, 1966.
[30] *Ibid.*, III-2308, Nanning broadcast of October 16, 1966.

for the absence of civil war in and the relative cleanliness of the Chinese town.[31]

The "China-Burma border people's friendship meeting" of December 16, 1956, was attended by 15,000 persons. Special significance was attached to the fact that peoples of the same nationality, known by different names on the two sides of the border, were brought together at the meeting: thus, Ching-p'o from China and Kachin from Burma; T'ai from China and Shan from Burma. They were said to have mingled together easily. It was noted that the Vice-chairman of the Te-hung T'ai and Ching-p'o autonomous *chou* and the Chairman of Burma's Kachin State, both of whom were at the meeting, had been schoolmates in their youth. Tao Ching-pan, the Te-hung *chou's* Chairman, encountered a relative—now an official in the Burmese government—at the meeting. A K'awa, formerly a prince in the area of the present-day Lan-tsang autonomous *hsien*, also met a relative at the meeting. All expressed the hope that the anticipated demarcation of the border would not prevent continued coming and going across the frontier.[32]

The meeting was attended by the Burmese and Chinese prime ministers, both of whom addressed the gathering. Prime Minister U Ba Swe declared that the effect of the meeting was to lay a cornerstone for the building of Sino-Burmese friendship. He added that the meeting would, specifically, give impetus to the development of intimacy between the peoples on the two sides of the border. Observing that the border was straddled by peoples of the same nationality, Prime Minister Chou En-lai said that the resulting trans-frontier ties were of great significance for Sino-Burmese friendship. Referring to China's large size in relation to Burma, he stated that the nationalities of Yunnan must make an even greater effort than those across the border in working toward closer relations between them. Both speakers referred to the Five Principles of Peaceful Coexistence.[33]

[31] Jan Myrdal, *Chinese Journey* (Boston, 1967), p. 142.
[32] *Yün-nan jih-pao*, December 17, 1956.
[33] *Ibid.*, December 17, 1956. For a discussion of the Mang-shih meeting in the context of Burmese politics and the negotiation of a Sino-Burmese

IMPACT OF THE SINO-BURMESE BORDER SETTLEMENT

Three years after the "China-Burma border people's friendship meeting" described above, another nationalities rally was held in Mang-shih. The purpose of the latter, convened on March 14, 1960, was to endorse the Sino-Burmese border agreement (*pien-chieh wen-t'i hsieh-t'ing*), together with a treaty of friendship and mutual non-aggression, which had been signed by the two governments in January. Ten thousand persons of various nationalities within the Te-hung T'ai and Ching-p'o autonomous *chou* were said to have attended the 1960 meeting. Prominent among the Burmese guests was the colonel in command of the adjacent military district, who took advantage of the occasion to hold discussions with his Chinese counterpart, the colonel in command of the T'eng-ch'ung military district (in southwest Yunnan). (In the winter of 1960/61 joint military operations were mounted by the PRC and Burma aimed at the final eradication of Nationalist forces in the Shan State.) It was noted in the Peking *People's Daily* that ever since the Mang-shih meeting of 1956, military authorities on the two sides of the frontier had been in regular contact.[34]

Addressing the March 1960 gathering, the Vice-chairman of the Te-hung *chou*, Wang Chih-hsiang, declared that the signing of the border agreement and the treaty of friendship were happy events for the peoples of the two countries. He asserted that the Sino-Burmese border question had been used by the imperialists to sow discord between the neighboring peoples of Burma and China, but that now the pre-existing ties of friendship had been restored. He said that, "As between our Te-hung T'ai and Ching-p'o autonomous *chou* and Burma's Kachin State and Shan State, the terrain is related, the villagers have a similar appearance, and many people are connected by family relationships." The visiting Burmese military commander spoke in a similar vein, noting in particular that im-

frontier settlement, see Dorothy Woodman, *The Making of Modern Burma* (London, 1962), especially pp. 530–531.

[34] *Jen-min jih-pao*, March 16, 1960.

perialist countries had made every effort to frustrate cooperation between neighboring states which adhered to socialism.[35]

Following a study of the Sino-Burmese border made by a
joint commission, a border treaty (*chung-mien pien-chieh
t'iao-yueh*) was signed in Peking by Chou En-lai and U Nu on
October 1, 1960 (the eleventh anniversary of the PRC). As the
two prime ministers were putting their signatures to the document, celebrations were being held among Yunnan's national
minority peoples living near the 2,000 kilometer-long frontier
with Burma. Participating in the festivities were residents of
the Te-hung T'ai and Ching-p'o autonomous *chou*; the Keng-
ma T'ai and K'awa autonomous *hsien*; the Ts'ang-yuan K'awa
autonomous *hsien*; the Meng-lien T'ai, Lahu, and K'awa autonomous *hsien*; and the Nu-chiang Lisu autonomous *chou*.
Several high government officials from Kunming took part in
these local celebrations, which were also attended by guests
from Burma. At the different places where the celebrations
were in progress, the people were said to have clapped and
cheered enthusiastically when the news was broadcast from
Peking that the treaty had been signed, and shouts of "Long
live the kindred friendship of the peoples of China and
Burma!" (*Chung-mien liang-kuo jen-min ch'in-ch'i pan ti yu-i
wan-sui!*) went up in various languages.[36]

On the afternoon of the following day (October 2) a festive
gathering took place in Kunming to mark the signing of the
border treaty. Official parties from both the Shan and Kachin
States were present, as were Yunnanese dignitaries including
the First Secretary of the provincial CCP Committee and the
Chairman of the Yunnan People's Government. The leaders
of the three autonomous *chou* of Te-hung, Hsi-shuang Pan-
na, and Nu-chiang also attended. There, too, was the Burmese
consul-general resident in Kunming. After listening to a number of speeches, the guests were rewarded by a feast.[37]

The border treaty became fully operative with the exchange
of instruments of ratification which took place when Chou

[35] *Ibid.*   [37] *Ibid.*, October 5, 1960.
[36] *Ibid.*, October 3, 1960.

En-lai visited Rangoon in January 1961. Later in the same month, the first anniversary of the preliminary border agreement was observed in Peking. Actually, it was the Sino-Burmese Treaty of Friendship and Mutual Non-aggression, signed at the same time as the border agreement, which received most of the attention. In an exchange of telegrams, U Nu and Chou En-lai spoke mainly of the treaty of friendship, but the border treaty was also mentioned, as were the more recently concluded trade agreements. Speaking at a celebration in Peking, Chou stated that the border was not one which separated but rather one which united the two countries.[38]

Following ratification, the border still had to be demarcated, and this process provided further opportunities for the demonstration of friendly feelings between the peoples on the two sides of the frontier. Thus, the joint teams engaged in setting up boundary posts along the border of Kengtung (the eastern region of the Shan State) and the Hsi-shuang Pan-na autonomous *chou* were said to have been warmly received when they visited Yun-ching-hung, the *chou's* capital, in March 1961. Amicable discussions were said to have been held concerning the work in progress along the frontier.[39]

U NU IN THE HSI-SHUANG PAN-NA

In April 1961 Prime Minister U Nu paid a ten-day visit to Yunnan, climaxed by a stay of two or three days in the Hsi-shuang Pan-na autonomous *chou*. His stay in the Hsi-shuang Pan-na coincided with the T'ai New Year. Accompanied by Chou En-lai, together with their wives and children, he watched the traditional dragon-boat festival on the Mekong River (*Lan-ts'ang chiang*), following which he attended a banquet given by Chao Ts'un-hsin, the *chou* Chairman. On the next day (April 15), the two Prime Ministers took part in another traditional T'ai New Year activity by joining a crowd of 5,000 people who were throwing water at each other in the

[38] *Ibid.*, January 28, 1961.
[39] *Yang-kuang jen-min pao* (Rangoon), March 2, 6, and 10, 1961; also, *Jen-min jih-pao*, March 6, 1961.

square of Yun-ching-hung. They were also said to have taken part in T'ai dancing.[40]

On April 16, Chou En-lai and U Nu issued a joint communiqué. It said that they had discussed the situation in Laos and the problem of Nationalist troops in Burma. The two leaders had also agreed on measures to implement the economic accords which had already been concluded between the two countries. The communiqué concluded with the statement that U Nu's visit to Yunnan had served to strengthen Sino-Burmese friendship.[41]

STRENGTHENING THE YUNNAN BORDER

Peking's relations with Rangoon have, as of this writing (early 1970), steadily hardened since U Nu's ouster by General Ne Win in 1962, when the former was on the point of making political concessions to Burma's minority peoples. This coup ended the halcyon days of Sino-Burmese intimacy described above, but it was not until 1967 that the cooling of relations between the two countries began to approach "cold war" temperatures. In June of that year Chinese students wearing Maoist badges were attacked in Rangoon. Burmese animosity against the entire Chinese community of over a quarter of a million people was soon manifested in dozens of Burmese towns and cities. Immediately thereafter clashes erupted in the north between Burmese and rebels said to be supported by the PRC. In the spring of 1969 a leading Burmese Communist, Thakin Ba Thein Tin, declared in a broadcast from Peking that the revolutionary forces in Burma enjoyed the backing of the PRC and the guidance of Chairman Mao's thought. Later in the same year, General Ne Win made it known that heavy fighting had occurred near the Sino-Burmese frontier and intimated that Chinese Communist troops had been involved.[42]

Although the worsening of the PRC's relations with Burma has heightened Chinese concern over the security of the

40 *Jen-min jih-pao*, April 15 and 16, 1961.
41 *Ibid.*, April 18, 1961.
42 *The New York Times*, March 22, July 25, and November 8, 1969.

Yunnan-Burma border, Kunming's appeals to the frontier peoples for greater efforts in support of the national defense have generally been keyed to US action in Vietnam. The task of mobilizing Yunnan's frontier peoples has been entrusted mainly to the PLA. Its role in national minority work in the province has already been discussed, but it has not, perhaps, been made clear that the PLA, over the years, formed permanent settlements and helped establish the state farms which gradually made their appearance on the frontier.[43] Furthermore, the role of the PLA units stationed on the Yunnan frontier was enhanced by the Cultural Revolution, a slogan of which was "learn from the PLA."

Although far less extensive than Kwangsi's, Yunnan does have a common frontier with North Vietnam. The Commander of the Kunming Military Region referred to this fact in a speech of September 1965:

> Yunnan province, being on the southwest border defense of the motherland, is connected with the DRV by land. We must regard support for the anti-American nation-saving struggle of the Vietnamese people as our own glorious and sacred mission. The people of the whole province should strengthen all work and be prepared to aid Vietnam and resist America with actual deeds.[44]

This theme was elaborated upon in a border work conference held half a year later. The conference, jointly convened by the Yunnan CCP Committee and the Kunming Military Region, adopted a resolution which said, in part:

> Our province, the great southwest gate of the motherland, is facing the serious threat of US imperialism expanding its war of aggression in Southeast Asia and trying to extend the flames of war to our territory. This demands that we maintain high vigilance, strengthen the concept of combat readiness, and speed up the building of the border areas. This is of extremely great importance in consolidating national defense

[43] BBC, *op. cit.*, III-1766, Peking broadcast of January 23, 1966, and *ibid.*, III-2054, Kunming broadcast of December 22, 1966.

[44] *Ibid.*, III-1969, Kunming broadcast of September 11, 1965.

and supporting the revolutionary struggles of the peoples of Southeast Asia. . . . Speeding up revolution and construction in the border areas, with the aim of building up a new socialist border, consolidating national defense, and supporting world revolution—these are the terms of reference and the starting point for us when considering border work.

Stressing the prominence of politics, a constant theme of the Cultural Revolution, the conference recommended that all cadres working in the border areas should take a copy of Mao's "Quotations" and a hoe when proceeding to the front line of agricultural production so as to bring Mao's thinking to the people. The resolution continued:

> The basic tasks of the border defense units are: to raise the great red flag of Mao Tse-tung's thinking, regard Chairman Mao's works as the supreme instructions on border defense work, unite and rely on the border peoples of various nationalities to safeguard and build up the border for a long time.[45]

Conclusion

Since the intensification of the United States' war effort in Vietnam in the early months of 1965 and the launching of China's Cultural Revolution in the following year, Yunnan and Kwangsi have become increasingly involved in an ever widening Southeast Asian conflict. The "summit conference of the Indochinese peoples," called in the spring of 1970 in response to the rightist coup which unseated Prince Sihanouk as the Cambodian Chief of State, dramatized the position of the two provinces as a bastion in an international conflict. The conference was held on the Yunnan frontier adjacent to the Lao-DRV border. At the meeting, which was attended by Prince Souphanouvong of the Pathet Lao, DRV Prime Minister Pham Van Dong, leaders of the National Liberation Front of South Vietnam, and Prince Sihanouk himself, Prime Minister Chou En-lai pledged Chinese support for the anti-US struggle in the several states of Indochina.[46] Only two years earlier, by way of

[45] Ibid., III-2130, Kunming broadcast of March 25, 1966.
[46] The New York Times, April 28, 29, 30 and May 1, 1970.

contrast, Red Guards raided the DRV Consulate in Nanning to register Maoist disapproval of the Paris peace talks.[47]

Instances of former Chiang adherents rallying to the cause of the motherland have in recent years become more commonplace than have incursions of Chiang "bandits" across the Yunnan frontier;[48] in the tense atmosphere which presently envelops the PRC's southern frontier, nevertheless, the Yunnan and Kwangsi authorities may be presumed to be in no mood to relax their vigilance with respect to the security of the non-Han areas.

National minority regions in the DRV, as well as in Yunnan, have been targets of foreign propaganda and manipulation. Hanoi radio admitted in 1959 that despite the fact that "the August Revolution began a new era for all nationalities . . . , nationality conflicts have not all been abolished." As a result, "the imperialists and their lackeys are resorting to every possible means to sow dissension among our nationalities. . . ." The broadcast went on to say that

> Lately, the enemy, taking advantage of the superstitions and hard life of a number of ethnic minorities and the shortcomings of our cadres in the application of policies, have created new conflicts with the hope of disturbing our rear.

The danger would remain, Hanoi said, so long as the minority peoples had not been fully integrated into the life of the country as a whole.[49] It was just a few months later that the draft of the 1960 Constitution, containing the important provisions concerning nationality relations alluded to in the previous chapter, began to be circulated.[50]

Whether or not the Cultural Revolution in China may be considered a response to the increased tension in the country's

---

[47] *The Times*, July 5, 1968.

[48] An instance of a Chiang warrior giving himself up in Yunnan and repenting of his past crimes was reported by the New China News Agency and carried in the *Ta-kung-pao* (Hong Kong) of March 11, 1967.

[49] BBC, *op. cit.*, V-835, Hanoi broadcast of January 4, 1959. My own talks with Americans in Saigon in early 1967 made it clear that the US-Diem side had, in fact, taken part in such activities.

[50] BBC, *op. cit.*, V-860, Hanoi broadcast of April 4, 1959.

international affairs, it tended to reinforce the stricter attitude toward the non-Han peoples of Yunnan and Kwangsi that had already been engendered by the critical frontier situation. The Buddhism of the T'ai in Yunnan came under vehement attack by Red Guards, and Red Guard factionalism in Kwangsi coincided to some degree with nationality divisions.[51] At least in comparison with the situation of minority peoples in adjacent states of the "free world," nevertheless, it would appear that the non-Han peoples have been rather successfully integrated into China's new polity and that the southern frontier regions of the PRC are not so vulnerable to outside penetration as they once were.

[51] Personal information gathered in 1967 from former residents of Yunnan and Kwangsi in the course of interviews held in Thailand and Hong Kong, respectively.

APPENDIX

AUTONOMOUS AREAS OF KWANGSI AND YUNNAN
ACCORDING TO THE *JEN-MIN SHOU-TS'E*
(*PEOPLE'S HANDBOOK*) OF 1965

I. The Kwangsi Chuang Autonomous Region contains eight autonomous *hsien*:

Lung-lin multinational   Ta-yao-shan Yao
Tu-an Yao   San-chiang T'ung
Pa-ma Yao   Lung-sheng multinational
Ta-miao-shan Miao   Tung-hsing multinational

II. Yunnan Province contains eight autonomous *chou* and fifteen autonomous *hsien*:

A. Autonomous *chou*:

Shih-shuang pan-na T'ai   Nu-chiang Lisu
Wen-shan Chuang and Miao   Ti-ch'ing Tibetan
Hung-ho Hani and Yi   Ta-li Pai
Te-hung T'ai and Ching-p'o   Ch'u-hsiung Yi

B. Autonomous *hsien*:

O-shan Yi   Meng-lien T'ai, K'awa, and Lahu
Lu-nan Yi   Hsi-meng K'awa
Ts'ang-yüan K'awa   Ho-k'ou Yao
Keng-ma T'ai and K'awa   P'ing-pien Miao
Li-chiang Na-hsi   Kung-shan Tu-lung and Nu
Ning-lang Yi   Wei-shan Yi and Hui
Chiang-ch'eng Hani and Yi   Nan-chien Yi
Lan-ts'ang Lahu

BIBLIOGRAPHY

A. NEWSPAPERS:

Ch'ang-chiang jih-pao (Hankow).
Chung-kuo Ch'ing-nien pao (Peking).
Chung-yang jih-pao (Taipei).
Hsin-hua yüeh-pao [monthly] (Peking).
Hsing-tao jih-pao (Hong Kong).
Jen-min jih-pao (Peking).
Kuang-hsi jih-pao (Nanning).
Kuei-chou jih-pao (Kueiyang).
Kung-shang jih-pao (Hong Kong).
Nan-fang jih-pao (Canton).
Nan-yang shang-pao (Singapore).
New York Herald Tribune (Paris edition).
The New York Times.
The Observer [weekly] (London).
Pien-chiang ch'ing-nien pao (Kunming).
Ta-kung jih-pao (Hong Kong).
Ta-kung-pao (Tientsin).
Ta-kung-pao (Peking).
Ta-kung-pao (Chungking).
T'ien-wen t'ai-pao (Hong Kong).
The Times (London).
Wen-hui-pao (Hong Kong).
Ya-chou jih-pao (Djakarta).
Yang-kuang jen-min pao (Rangoon).
Yün-nan jih-pao (Kunming).

B. JOURNALS:

Bulletin de l'Ecole Francaise d'Extreme-Orient (Hanoi, Saigon).
Journal of the Burma Research Society (Rangoon).

Journal of the Siam Society (Bangkok).
Min-tsu t'uan-chieh (Nationalities unity). (Peking).
Min-tsu yen-chiu (Nationalities research). (Peking).

C. RADIO BROADCASTS AND WIRE SERVICES:

BBC Monitoring Service. *Summary of World Broadcasts* (Reading, Berks.). 1959–1966.
Chung-kuo hsin-wen (Peking, Canton).

D. BOOKS AND ARTICLES:

A Yün-pien. *Hsi-shuang pan-na ho t'ai-tsu* (The Sip-song Pan-na and the T'ai people). Peking, 1961.
Beauclair, Inez de. "Ethnic Groups." *A General Handbook of China.* Human Relations Area Files, New Haven, circa 1956.
Bruk, S.I. *Karta Narodov Kitaia, MNR i Korei.* Moscow, 1959.
Burchett, Wilfred. *Mekong Upstream.* Hanoi, 1957.
Central Intelligence Agency. *Communist China Map Folio.* Washington, 1967.
Chandrasckhar, S. *China's Population.* Hong Kong, 1959.
Chang Chi-yun (ed.). *National Atlas of China,* Vol. IV: *South China.* Taipei, 1962.
Chang Chi-yun. "Climate and Man in China." *Annals of the Association of American Geographers,* XXXVI, 1 (March 1946), pp. 44–73.
Chang Chi-jen. "The Minority Groups of Yunnan and Chinese Expansion into Southeast Asia." Unpublished Ph.D. dissertation, University of Michigan, 1956.
Chang Chih-i. *Chung-kuo ko-ming ti min-tsu wen-t'i ho min-tsu cheng-ts'e chiang-hua (t'i-kang)* (A discussion of the national question in the Chinese revolution and of actual nationalities policy [draft]). Peking, 1956.
Chang Hsia-min. *Pien-chiang wen-t'i yü pien-chiang chien-she* (Frontier questions and frontier development). Taipei, 1958.
Common Program of the Chinese People's Political Consultative Conference (CPPCC). *The Important Documents of the First Plenary Session of the* CPPCC. Peking, 1949.
Constitution of the People's Republic of China (PRC). *Documents of the First Session of the First National Congress of the* PRC, Peking, 1955.
Cressey, George B. *Asia's Lands and Peoples.* New York, 1963.
——— *China's Geographic Foundations.* New York and London, 1934.
Chu-shou pien-chiang ti wei-kuo chan-shih (The nation's defenders stationed on the frontiers). Peking, 1953.
DeFrancis, John. "National and Minority Policies." *Annals of the*

American Academy of Political and Social Science, 277 (September 1951).

Dodd, William C. *The Tai Race.* Cedar Rapids, Mich., 1923.

Dubbs, H.H. "The Concept of Unity in China." Stanley Pargellis (ed.). *The Quest for Political Unity in World History.* Washington, 1944, pp. 3–19.

Duke, Pensri. *Les Relations entre la France et la Thailande aux XIXeme Sicole.* Bangkok, 1962.

Economic Geography of the South China Region. JPRS (US Department of Commerce, Joint Publications Research Service) No. 14954 (a translation of Sun Ching-chih. *Hua-nan ti-ch'ü ching-chi ti-li.* Peking, 1959).

Economic Geography of the Southwest China Region. JPRS No. 15069 (a translation of Sun Ching-chih. *Hsi-nan ti-ch'ü ching-chi ti-li.* Peking, 1960).

Fairbank, John K. and Teng Ssu-yu. *Ch'ing Administration.* Cambridge, Mass., 1960.

Fall, Bernard B. *The Viet-Minh Regime.* Ithaca, N.Y., 1954.

Fitzgerald, C.P. *China, A Short Cultural History.* London, 1965.

———— *The Tower of Five Glories.* London, 1941.

General Program of the People's Republic of China (PRC) *for the Implementation of Regional Autonomy for the Nationalities. Policy Towards Nationalities of the* PRC. Peking, 1953.

Gourou, Pierre. "The Development of Upland Areas in China." *The Development of Upland Areas in the Far East.* Vol. I. New York, 1949.

———— "Land Utilization in Upland Areas of Indochina." *Ibid.* Vol. II. New York, 1951.

———— *L'Asie.* Paris, 1953.

Graham, David C. "The Miao." *Journal of the West China Border Research Society,* IX (1937).

Harvey, G.E. "The Wa People of the Burma-China Frontier." *St. Antony's Papers,* No. 2 (1957), pp. 126–135.

Hermann, Albert. *Historical and Commercial Atlas of China.* Taipei, 1964.

Hudson, G.F. "The Nationalities of China." *St. Antony's Papers,* No. 7 (1960), pp. 51–61.

Jen-min shou-ts'e (People's Handbook). Peking, 1965.

Kuang-hsi chuang-tsu tzu-ch'ih-ch'ü (The Kwangsi Chuang Autonomous Region). Peking, 1958.

Kuang-hsi ko-ming hui-i-lu (Memoirs of the Revolution in Kwangsi). Nanning, 1958.

Kunstadter, Peter (ed.). *Southeast Asian Tribes, Minorities, and Nations.* 2 vols. Princeton, 1967.

Lattimore, Owen. *Inner Asian Frontiers of China.* New York, 1940.

Leach, E.R. *Political Systems of Highland Burma.* London, 1964.

LeBar, Frank M. Gerald C. Hickey, and John C. Musgrave. *Ethnic Groups of Mainland Southeast Asia.* New Haven, 1964.

Li Chi. *The Formation of the Chinese People.* Cambridge, Mass., 1928.

Lin Yueh-hua. "The Minority Peoples of Yunnan." *China Reconstructs,* X, 12 (December 1961).

Lin Yueh-hwa. *The Lola of Liang Shan.* New Haven, 1961.

Liu Shao-ch'i. "Report on the Draft Constitution of the People's Republic of China (PRC)." *Documents of the First Session of the First National Congress of the PRC.* Peking, 1955.

Ma Ch'ang shou. "Shao-shu min-tsu wen-t'i" (The national minority question). *Min-tsu hsüeh yen-chiu chi-k'an* (Ethnological Research), Vol. VI. Chungking, 1948.

Mangrai, Sao Saimons. *The Shan States and the British Annexation.* Ithaca, N.Y., 1965.

Myrdal, Jan. *Chinese Journey.* Boston, 1967.

Nguyen Khak Vien (ed.). *Mountain Regions and National Minorities In the DR of Vietnam.* Hanoi, 1968.

Pipes, Richard. *The Formation of the Soviet Union.* Cambridge, Mass., 1957.

Roux, Henri. "Quelque Minorities Ethnique de Nord-Indochine." *France-Asie,* X, 92–93 (January–February 1954). Saigon.

Savina, F.M. *Histoire des Miao.* Hong Kong, 1930.

Scott, J. George, and J.P. Hardiman. *Gazeteer of Upper Burma and the Shan States.* 5 vols. Rangoon, 1900/01.

Seidenfaden, Eric. *The Thai Peoples,* Bangkok, 1963.

Shaheen, Samad. *The Communist (Bolshevik) Theory of National Self-Determination.* The Hague and Bandung, 1956.

T'ang Chen-tsung. *Chung-kuo shao-shu min-tsu hsin mien-mao* (The new appearance of China's national minorities). Peking, 1953.

Tang, Peter S.H. *Communist China Today.* 2 vols. Washington, 1961.

Wiens, Herold J. *China's March Toward the Tropics.* Hamden, Conn., 1954.

Willoughby, Westel W. *Foreign Rights and Interests in China.* Baltimore, 1920.

Woodman, Dorothy. *The Making of Modern Burma.* London, 1962.

Young, Gordon. *The Hill Tribes of Northern Thailand.* Bangkok, 1966.

INDEX